Playing Out
Swings and Roundabouts

By Paul Douglas Lovell

Playing Out: Swings and Roundabouts

Cover by Paul Douglas Lovell

Editing and formatting by editing.zone

Proofreading by editing.zone and @paginginferno

Printed Edition License Notes

Disclaimer

This book is a work of non-fiction based on the life, experiences and recollections of the author. In some limited cases names of people, places, dates, sequences or the detail of events have been changed (solely) to protect the privacy of others. The author states that, except in minor respects not affecting the substantial accuracy of the work, the contents of this book are true.

Acknowledgements and thanks

To Michael Thommen for his unwavering love and support.
Deirdre O'Connell who guided and encouraged me to educate myself.
My editor Stephanie Dagg.

Dedicated to my father; Douglas Frank Lovell

Chapter One: Meet Paul And His Dad

Perhaps, as he's so often heard, scraggly-haired Paul really is a magnet for misfortune. Maybe trouble does attract trouble because, following close at his heels, pursuing classmates chant, *"He's a tramp, he's a tramp, he's a tramp."* It begins with a request from Paul to play and a swift refusal on the grounds of no tramps allowed. Then a second plea, voiced in a most cajoling manner, which is met with a shove from Anthony Hayes, a few giggles and the impromptu chorus of *"He's a tramp,"* which quickly escalates. Backing away from the jeers, this pack mentality terrifies the six-year-old and his pulse races. He flees, and a chase around the infant's playground ensues.

Paul bolts past his classroom window. Allies Bobby and Shane, members of his gang the Anti-Creeps, look on from inside. Sentenced to playtime detention for some earlier transgression means they cannot support him. He has no idea how to dispel the chase, which consists of both boys and girls. Under normal circumstances, with Bobby and Shane by his side, this wouldn't have happened, they being the roughest, most boisterous rascals in Green Class. But it is happening now, and he has no plan other than to run as fast as he can. At the entrance to the junior children's playground, he sees one of his older brothers, Darren, who advises, no, *orders* him to hit them. So grabbing a fist full of the first child's jumper, Paul pulls Barry, who bites, towards him and punches him on the nose. He does the same to Anthony Hayes and then Derek Cole and the pitchfork mob then hastily disperse.

***

Paul comes from a broken home with boarded-up windows, peeling wallpaper and, on the floors that *are* covered, threadbare carpets. His mother abandoned the family six weeks after his birth. Leaving "the three eldest" boys, Mark, Jason and Darren, and the "two little 'uns", a girl named Carole and new-born Paul, in the hands of their lorry-driver father. He is a tall man who carries no extra fat on his slender frame. Dark-skinned, tanned like Aladdin. His origins are unknown, which leaves lots of fantastic possibilities for Paul to ponder. His dad often mentions his past, tall tales about crossing the Gobi desert on foot. He says a lot of things. He talks to his children, shouts too, but generally talks. He takes the time to explain and speaks with authority. Paul's dad is strong-willed with a unique perspective of what is right and wrong: there are never any shades of grey. More a thinker than a feeler, he doesn't believe in mollycoddling his children.

Love is more a concept than a product, an auricular experience implied or derived from one fact. The children accept they are loved because, despite the noisy chaos that accompanies five, their father, unlike their mother, has stuck around and hasn't placed them into state care. He has often unnerved his wide-eyed children with horror stories of his own tragic childhood, being beaten and terribly mistreated in what he refers to as "the cottage homes". In jest, and occasionally frustration, he sometimes threatens to shove them all in a home for a single moment of peace. However, a slight twitch at the corner of his mouth always betrays the mischievous smiles that he tries to hide.

Paul's father, who was raised by nuns from birth, has no experience of a family life and struggles to cope. But cope he does. Determined to save his children from the wicked clutches of orphanage nuns, he takes whatever help and advice the welfare workers offer. It was under their instruction that, when his estranged wife decided she wanted to take ten-week-old Paul after all, he was handed over. Some weeks later washerwoman-gossip made its way across the back garden fence. News that Paul's mother, who happened to be newly pregnant, had moved on leaving Paul with some random family. It infuriated Paul's father to hear that this juicy piece of tittle-tattle had been doing the rounds for some time and so, without delay and with little disturbance, Paul was back within the family unit.

In those first years finding responsible childminders eluded Paul's father. There were no close friends or relations he could call upon for help. He discovered that he couldn't depend on the goodwill of local babysitters, and even those who charged a fee were somewhat unreliable. Paul can recall his sister Carole, in the absence of the childminder, tumbling from the dining-room table. He retains this cloudy image, complete with sound, as one of his earliest memories, perhaps because it was partly his fault. The pair of them, sitting on top of the table squabbling. She grabbing for a wooden donkey head, part of a condiment set, and following it over the edge as it rolled to the ground. At first she didn't cry. Then she saw blood dot the floor.

After which she rattled a whole row of houses with her howling screams. Another teenage babysitter brazenly displayed a love-bite on her neck. She saw nothing wrong with bragging about getting Mark, who was only seven years old, to supply it. So after many letdowns and dodgy incidents, Paul's pragmatic father concluded it would be best to resign from his job to become a stay-at-home parent.

Be under no illusion that Paul's father is a saint. Like most parents he has good and bad moods and, when his patience is tried, he disciplines his children the old-fashioned way: a spanking on the bottom, a bare bottom, swiftly administered in the schoolyard. Served in front of classmates, teachers and parents, it's a stinging reminder of whose word is final. Fortunately the notion of embarrassment, just like Paul, is still undeveloped, although next time, he will come when called. Figuring out parental logic is never easy, and for a cheeky child born in the year of the monkey, differentiating playful behaviour from being naughty is also tricky. Perhaps stumbling down the stairs and then receiving a smack for crying is deserved. It is quite possible, although Paul doesn't remember if a verbal warning preceded the event, nevertheless a soothing hug from a soft-eyed mother isn't the way of things in his rowdy house.

To help neutralise some of the household turbulence, the children's father enforces continuity and a strict regime. Some house rules are deeply scored into the rock that is Paul's brain. Bed at six-thirty, never hit girls and absolutely no buts. Mark, Jason and Darren are allowed to stay up later than Carole and Paul: for them, when the Tom and Jerry cartoon ends so does their day.

One surety they all know is if their dad isn't sitting in his favourite chair doing a crossword puzzle or playing chess against himself, he can be found having a swift pint or two at the Beckley Tavern, one of his regular boozers. The pub, his sanctuary from all the stress and noise, is strictly to maintain his sanity and the mild ale he consumes is viewed as a measured essential. Money is always tight, so all non-essentials like sweets, pocket money, school trips and birthday presents are privileges afforded only to two-parent families. Christmas is the only exception: the whole family agrees that is most definitely an essential.

Chapter Two: Toddler Paul

Toddler Paul has a tendency to lose track and wander off. In the supermarket he looks up to discover that the fistful of trouser leg scrunched within his hand does not belong to his father but to another towering shopper. On a trip to the local park with one of his brothers he continues to wander straight through it and out the other side. Somehow he manages to cross a busy road and is found some time later in Bessy's sweetshop near St Jude's Church, which is a good twenty-minute walk away. When asked by a policeman where he lives, he responds with the line "In a car." Stuck in a notion, all questions asked of him are answered with the same three words. Rough and scruffy, it may be assumed he belongs to a traveling family or perhaps he's simply angling for a ride in the police car that he sees parked outside the shop. He is successful in that. After a bit of detective work by PC Spoon, the local bobby, Paul is given a ride in a police car and, with two flicks of the siren-switch, he arrives home with a pocketful of sweets.

On school days he hears the moans and groans of the three eldest asking if they really have to go to school. "I can't afford to feed you if you stay home," is his father's general response. School lunches, which are free to one-parent families, provide much of the nourishment lacking in their regular diet of beans on toast and jam sandwiches. Hence, as his brothers and sister toddle off to school, Paul waves goodbye, glad that he doesn't have to go too.

Living in a house full of boisterous kids all vying for attention, Paul is delighted to have his dad all to himself even if it is all *peace and quiet*. With the house empty, and his father mulling over the news in yesterday's paper, the clock ticks so much louder. Paul must occupy himself. Riding the creaky living room door is one way. Hands clamped on both handles, toes gripping the recessed panelling, Paul hangs there calling to his father, desperate to be pushed before his feet slip off. Not today. Today his father is short with him tells him to get down before he breaks something.

Although he's not really meant to, Paul, avoiding the two loose rails, climbs the staircase bannister all the way up to the top of the house, without touching a single step. Then he crocodiles his way down on his stomach. In the kitchen, using a high stool that has two steps attached, he climbs onto the tabletop and opens a cupboard to peer in. He retrieves a block of gummy red cubes wrapped in see-through plastic. A strawberry jelly, which he takes into the bathroom just off the kitchen to hide behind the feet of the cast iron tub. This isn't the first time he's done this, in fact it's the third. Two previous jellies were discovered by his father whilst mopping the floor and returned to the kitchen. When the family were gathered and questioned, everyone denied hiding them. Paul, presumed to be too small, wasn't even asked, which is just as well as he'd forgotten he'd done it.

With the others around it's difficult keeping track of all his memories. However, he does have a few favourites that are too precious to forget. Paul used to bathe in the kitchen sink. His dad would tease that if he didn't pluck him to safety Paul would be sucked down the plughole. He enjoyed splashing his feet in a panic before being scooped into the air. Sometimes he'd sit watching and waiting as his father attempted to bake a cake, eager to lick the sugary mess left on the wooden spoon. He remembers crouching behind the sofa, being shushed as he and his dad played hide and seek with the rent-man. The man would mill about outside the window, attempting to peer into the gloom of an unlit room and call through the letterbox. Paul wasn't permitted to move until he'd gone.

One time his dad became locked out of the house with Paul trapped inside. In those days Paul wasn't able to reach the latch. He barely remembers the incident except when prompted by his father, who proudly recounts the event. The calm way in which Paul followed instructions to drag the stool all the way from the kitchen and across the hall. Climbing up and, after a struggle, twisting the stiff catch to open the front door. Thus saving a window from being smashed and earning him a lot of praise.

Sometimes, like today, Paul gets to go places. Grasping tightly to a gigantic finger that looks and smells a bit like a cigar, he trots alongside, desperately trying to keep pace. Paul's dad walks at an incredible speed. On some occasions, this being one, they catch a double-decker bus. As he scrambles up the enormous stairs to the top deck, he knows that no matter how severely the bus jerks or turns, his dad is there to catch him should stumble backwards. Paul likes to sit at the front where he uses the handrail to steer the bus along the route. He isn't supposed to block the view; his dad tells him that it says so on a notice. Still Paul can't resist leaning over to have a sneak peek into the periscope of viewing mirrors that allow the driver to keep an eye on the upstairs passengers. Paul jerks back his head and sits somewhat nicely after he catches a glimpse of the driver's glance. Mental fidgeting soon commences, a battle between *should I* and *best not* wavers. Paul understands it is wrong, and he returns to steering the bus.

Travelling on straight roads Paul mostly feels fine but on bendy journeys his stomach churns and his face loses all traces of pigment. Tingling hands and a growing weakness in his joints, he is beginning to recognise the early signs of travel sickness just as it is time to alight the bus. Rushing through the lively town centre in order to catch a second bus, Paul projectile vomits with such force it splashes back from the gutter, splattering his ankles. A handkerchief, still warm from his father's pocket, wipes away traces of dribble. Paul's dad has a tendency to apply more pressure than is required and what in reality is a soft cotton fabric suddenly takes on the scrubbing qualities of unrefined sackcloth.

Paul's father leads him towards the town's monument, a stately prince astride a magnificent horse. They take a seat at the base of its stone plinth. A short break which allows Paul's stomach to unfold and his complexion to return to a more natural shade. Paul's dad lights a cigarette and it isn't long before Paul is scrambling about the statue, peering up into the flaring nostrils of the beast which appears to be glaring at him in annoyance. Perhaps offended by the pungent waves of vomit being released around its feet. The stench will cling to Paul for the rest of the day.

The second bus journey, which is moderately winding, doesn't seem to bother Paul. He falls asleep with his head resting on his father's lap until they reach their destination.

Soaring high into the sky is a block of flats. Paul has seen these colossal high-rise structures before as there are three towers quite close to the school his siblings attend. Also Mary, Mungo and Midge, characters from a cartoon show, live on the seventh floor in a tall block and Paul particularly likes to watch them ride in the lift. Just like Midge, Paul needs to be picked up in order to press the button to take them up to the ninth floor. A smell of emulsion paint dominates the corridor, and it mingles with the odour that is coming from Paul's clothes.

They enter the home of a heavily-perfumed, old lady. She says hello to Paul but talks to him no more. As she busies herself in the kitchen, Paul's dad looks out of the window and Paul scopes the room. The place, furnished mainly with an echo, contains little in the way of comfort. A two-person table with chairs, a leather sofa and a television. A collection of cardboard boxes stacked against one wall is all the room possesses in the way of interest. Paul is too short to see above the windowsill so his dad pulls over one of the chairs. Paul clambers on to it to marvel at the view. Tree tops sway beneath him. Green patches of land and buildings stretch out as far as his eyes can see. Scoring through them, cars creep along snake-like pathways. Best of all, people so tiny Paul feels he could blow them all away with a mighty huff and a puff. Left at the window to daydream over the scene, his father takes a seat on the sofa. The clink of cutlery and crocks attracts Paul's attention. His dad and the old woman sip tea and talk. There is no cake but Paul does get to drink the overspill of tea from his dad's saucer. The meeting doesn't last long; in fact, it comes to a rather abrupt end. Paul knows his dad is upset as he can see a watery glaze within his reflective eyes hardening to ice. The lady has asked him not to call again, frightened that her neighbours will think he is one of her gentlemen clients. This, the final attempt on his father's part to include his own estranged mother in the life of her grandchildren, has failed. Paul, none the wiser he's just met his grandmother, is smitten when his dad buys him a tube of chocolate Smarties on the way home. It has a dark blue lid with a letter B on it, or maybe it is a D. Preschool Paul doesn't yet know his letters.

Chapter Three: Home Life

Paul's family live in a back street, a lengthy cul-de-sac with a large circle at the bottom. From outside number twenty-two, his house, the two little 'uns, Carole and Paul, are not supposed to step beyond the two nearest lampposts. One is down the hill outside number thirty, the other up, at number fourteen. A third lamppost situated midway between the two, Paul claims as his own because it stands just outside his garden gate. On dark nights, it casts a glow upon the walls of his bedroom, the primary light source for a room without a bulb.

Hugging the lamppost, twirling round and around and around until dizzy. Following the embossed swirls that decorate the base with his finger. Countless failed attempts to shimmy up it, so he can sit on the t-bar beneath the bulb as he's seen bigger kids do, all hold his attention for a while. Frustratingly he can only watch as the three eldest, Mark, Jason and Darren, scoot off, vanishing out of sight off on some wild, mysterious adventure. Paul's pleas to tag along are always ignored. His dad and brothers all agree that he is too little and must stay where he can be seen.

Somewhat liberated from social conventions, working-class children are often allowed to play out unsupervised. This provides some parents an opportunity to nip down to their local pub for a swift half. There are always enough prying eyes about in a street like Paul's. Chatting at the gate posts opposite, two old women while away most of the day, smoking cigarettes and sharing stories. Paul's amused father speaks fondly about how Paul used to spend hours sitting with them listening to their gossip. Paul feels pride whenever he hears stories about himself and he can still picture this one, first hand.

Other than not having to go to school, Paul sees no additional bonus for being the youngest in his family. Instead he receives a booby prize: his sister Carole. She is currently sitting in the middle of the road using a lollipop stick to dislodge a stubborn piece of bubble gum. She's been told not to do it, knows that it is dirty, even Paul knows that, but she eats it anyway. Carole is a year and a half older than Paul. She is not at all girly, probably because she lives in a house full of boys. A tomboy with goofy teeth and messy brown hair. Like her father, she is strong-willed and constantly battles him, resulting in painful howls and slapped legs whenever he tries to comb out her tangled tresses.

She is a strange sister. A short while back she threw a *half-ender*, a piece of a house brick, at Paul's face. It hit him above the eye making it pour with blood. The scab has not long healed. Perhaps, when she pulled back her arm, she'd meant to drop the brick behind her shoulder. Only pretending to throw it. Maybe she simply mistimed the letting go part, although Paul didn't view it that way. He remembers her standing in front of him and lobbing something hard at his head. Regardless, she received a proper good hiding from their dad for doing it.

Not to be outdone by their brothers, Carole and Paul go on a mini adventure of their own, venturing all the way to the circle at bottom of the cul-de-sac. With a pencil and a notepad they go from door to door as Carole copies down all the numbers they find. Obviously the importance of listing house numbers is worth the risk of them being sent to bed without any tea. They remember to avoid number twenty-nine, Mr Carlson's, the house with all the flowers. When Carole and Paul were a little younger, too young to know better, they picked some of his beautiful blooms. He was livid when they knocked at his door to ask if he wanted to buy any. He yelled, "Get up your own end, ya cheeky bleeders," adding, as they dropped the flowers to scarper away, "I'll tell your dad. I know who you are." On that occasion they ran back to the sanctuary of their lamppost and nothing else came of it. Mr Carlson seems to have forgotten but Carole hasn't and, not wanting to remind him, they scuttle by to the next front door, number twenty-seven. Paul notices, like on his front door, there are a lot of twos on Carole's list.

***

In the theme of twos, Paul's father currently owns two pianos. Both are out tune but that doesn't matter as he can play the opening section of a piece entitled 'Chopsticks' and nothing more. The family also have two dogs. Blackie, who belongs to Bill, their some-of-the-time lodger, is an old blind Labrador with a tendency to drop smelly farts, and Podge is a hairy mongrel that likes to fight. They too are allowed to roam freely, which they do, covering great distances. Podge guides Blackie across roads and supposedly, it is said, catches the bus to town. Blackie, being quite fat, makes a great pillow up until a point: a certain level of toxicity. When Blackie blows, everybody in the house knows.

Another of Paul's younger day memories includes the dogs sitting by the piano. "A bit for you, a bit for you and a bit for me." Paul recalls his dad laughing at the sight of them. Standing atop the piano stool, the three of them taking turns to slather-dribble all over a Curly Wurly, a chocolate chewy bar. The stretched strands of toffee dripping with saliva must have looked a right sight, especially after several rounds of being tugged from the determined grip of canine teeth.

What a mega Christmas that was, a lifetime ago, which in reality was only eleven months back. Paul received a white plastic horse with wheels, a pedal-car and a cuddly lifelike chimpanzee. The car never really pedalled properly and the steering wheel soon snapped off, leaving a jagged stump that tore at his flesh. But the horse was excellent. The incline on Paul's street is steep, which made it possible to gallop almost all the way to the bottom without stopping. He had such fun, reaching incredible speeds. Paul's brothers showed an interest in him, for a short time, until the inevitable. Each collision bent the wheel axle that little bit more: the horse began to hobble and eventually became completely lame. It was put out to pasture in the back garden where it remains in amongst the weeds.

Weather permitting, Paul occupies his time giving shoulder rides to Monkey, his chimpanzee. There's a squabble over ownership, Darren tormenting Paul by insisting that they had swapped toys and Monkey now belongs to him. Tugging one hand each they tear it apart, then squabble further over its head. Which, after tears, telling tales and smacked bottoms, Paul rightfully gains full custody of. Hollowed out, the head becomes a Planet of the Apes-style mask, and after his father ties knots in the open ends of the limbs to contain the stuffing, Paul makes good use of the slugging arms. He swings them about, clobbering Darren hard across the back of his head, producing a rather loud clonk. This isn't done with malice, Paul simply complies to a slapstick urge, a notion that flashes through his mind, one influenced by cartoons. This action makes everyone laugh, including their father. Darren, unable to retaliate, doesn't laugh. However, later that day, he bets Paul that he can't fit a ping-pong ball into his mouth. A challenge Paul easily accomplishes, albeit at a salty price. Paul has fallen foul of a dastardly prank. Darren roars with laughter. "Errr, it's got wee on it."

Paul spits the ball out and tries to clean his tongue by licking his woollen sleeve, which is even more unpleasant. Devious Darren had dipped the ball into a bowl of Paul's pee. Paul has been suffering with a painful, itchy swelling of the toes. He has chilblains and has been urinating into a bowl in the bathroom because his father believes that soaking his chilblains in urine will alleviate some of the irritation. It isn't in any way a miracle cure but Paul feels a little relief whilst bathing his feet.

As toys never last long in their house, other, creative forms of play naturally develop. Making mud-pies, digging holes and collecting unlikely treasures, such as bottle tops and ring-pulls. Paul enjoys crawling about and hiding beneath the wooden pigeon pen in the back garden. He much prefers to be underneath where it is dark, musty and moist, if not a tad dangerous due to protruding nails, than inside it where the dusty air makes him wheeze and sneeze. Lured by a feast of woodlice and slugs, it is a haven for passing amphibians. He sometimes comes across one whilst under there.

Paul's dad is a member of a pigeon club. On most weekends during the racing season his best birds compete. He boasts that, unlike his rivals, he has never bought a single pigeon, yet still wins many races. These victories are rewarded at the end of the season with trophies and cash prizes. Therefore the health and welfare of his pigeons is highly important. Darren, who is considered to be *Daddy's pet*, is permitted to assist his father and gets to tag along, although this is mainly on training days. As money is involved racing is taken seriously. On race days the children are banished from using the garden, and woe betide the forgetful child who rushes around the side of the house, scaring away the birds. For the eldest three it is a good time to request playing further afield than the local back park in places like the Woodlands, down the canal or over Windsor Park playing fields. The two little 'uns have to make do with the street.

Today is a race day. Carole is once again logging door numbers and Paul is inside. He's peering out of an upstairs window overlooking the back garden. The silence of an empty house is broken. *Cha, cha, cha, cha, cha.* Paul's dad stands by the back doorstep, his eyes searching the skies, whilst rattling a metal can containing dried corn. Between each strain of five shakes he pauses a moment and then adds a chanted refrain of "C'mon, c'mon, c'mon then, c'mon." He repeats the sequence over and over again until a pigeon eventually flutters from the sky to land on a nearby rooftop.

Paul watches his dad scatter some grains near pen's entrance to entice the bird down. The pigeon appears overly cautious and flaps over to perch on a chimney pot. It cranes its neck scanning the vicinity with a beady eye. Casting suspicious glances, it sees the man shaking a can and the boy standing on the sill behind the glass window. Paul can barely make out the feed on the ground. He has heard that a pigeon can see for miles and miles and wonders why the bird refuses to be swayed. There are no cats about, Blackie and Podge are out in the street and the neighbouring gardens look deserted. When spooked, this coaxing method of tin rattling and calling requires a lot of patience. Paul's dad possesses a finite amount which, to be honest, isn't a great deal especially when every minute that passes is a potential loss of income. Normally the pigeon, hungry after a lengthy flight, would circle around once or twice, land on a roof then, seeing the food being sprinkled, swoop down to eat. Paul's dad would then toss a few morsels in the shed entrance and usher the racer further inside whilst sliding the door closed behind him. Once cornered and caught he would remove from its feet a rubber ring: a fat, elasticated band stamped with an identity number, allocated before the race. This is then enclosed inside a tiny metal canister that resembles a sewing thimble. A clock that can't be opened or adjusted without a master key, one guarded by the chief timekeeper of the club, waits to receive the thimble. Inserted into a small hole it is secured within a chamber deep inside the clock and the time is registered.

Mr Pearce, Bob to his racing colleagues and who lives nearby on the main road, also keeps pigeons. His clock has a slight time difference, adjusted to allow for variations in distance. So precise are these calculations, every minute is counted when determining the winner. As most of the family know it's all very serious and if, at this moment, Paul's father happens to look up at the window behind him, Paul would surely be taught a lesson for a second time.

***

To toughen up the boys, Paul's dad positively encourages physical fighting. Not exactly a pit-bull way of life, but on rainy afternoons, baiting one another in wrestling matches, orchestrated by their father, is conducted on the living room floor. Bog standard life coaching in many working-class households of the seventies. Everyone bar Carole wrestles. She just cheers and jumps about, appearing a lot more frenzied than anyone fighting. Darren may be small but he whips about like a vicious terrier and generally gets the better of everyone, even Mark, the eldest. Frustrations inevitably flare up and, every once in a while, hurt pride bubbles over into tears. Strictly forbidden, this type of crying is swiftly rewarded with something to cry about, putting an end to what should have been a bit of rough and tumble.

Name calling and teasing are also advocated. Toughening to protect their core. Their father believes it encourages them to suppress their upset emotions should children make fun of them. He frowns upon them showing weakness, and if they don't hit back when punched? Well, knowing what will happen once their dad finds out prevents any cheek-turning. Paul always adheres to his dad's commands. "If the teacher hits you across the head, just say... *Don't hit me across the head or I'll be as stupid as you.*" It takes a lot of guts and full control over quivering lips to deliver such a lengthy sentence. Yet it is doable because it has been done by both Jason and Darren. The children generally do as they are ordered. However, by default, all the things their father fails to forbid are allowed.

Chapter Four: Yellow Class

As much as Paul enjoys staying home, time inevitably ticks on. Paul's introduction to St Jude's Catholic School begins in the spring following his fourth birthday.

Mark is first to leave the house on this particular morning. He attends senior school, which is much further away, and dashes out the door before Paul is fully dressed. Darren and Jason scoot off next, glad to be relieved of Carole, a burden that normally tags along. Carole, together with Dad, accompany Paul on his first walk to school. There are no tantrums at the school gates. His father, eager to rush off, delivers them to the top of the road and watches them enter the playground before waving goodbye.

Paul attends Yellow Class, which is split into two groups. The older children of five going on six, taught by Mrs Coutts, occupy the desks and have to sit up straight, pay attention and raise their hands before talking. They also use pencils and exercise books. The younger kids, watched over by Miss Bishop, the classroom assistant, seem to have it easier, sprawling about the red carpet in the story time area. The smell of wax crayons and Plasticine within the room acts like a stimulus to Paul. He is itching to explore all the brightly-coloured toys, to enter the Wendy house and make castles in the sandpit. At this early stage of his schooling, excluding social skills there are no difficult lessons. In circle-time they sing a morning song, 'Incy Wincy Spider', change the cards on the weather display and adjust the calendar. They count up to ten and, much to the children's delight, back down again, the best part coming after "three, two, one" when they all jump into the air shouting "Blast off!" and making rocket noises.

All children wear plimsolls or socks in class; shoes are not allowed. So, shortly before the ringing of morning break-time bell, the children are sent to the cloakroom to change for outdoor play. When the bell sounds, the doors are flung open and out pour Yellow, Blue and Green classes, roaring and screaming into the playground. Carole is amongst them but Paul doesn't want to play with her. Instead he runs around with Bobby and Shane, the most boisterous of his new classmates. Bobby, a blond Irish lad, is smaller than Paul yet much tougher. Bobby can do boxing and claims to be able to fight anyone. Shane is also Irish. A dark-haired, stocky, thick-headed boy with a hard temper, he is also a good fighter. Unbeknown to Paul, the impressions made in these early moments will be chiseled deep into the foundations of his new school. A scale that measures popularity and, subsequently, the level of acceptance within the micro society that is his class. By the time the whistle blows for them to line up, they are well on their way to becoming friends.

After the exertion of recess comes a refreshing drink of milk. At home Paul never has real milk. It is considered a luxury beyond their means so he relishes this creamy supply of liquid calcium. Slurping loudly, the children's drinking straws chase every last drop around and around the base of the bottle. Much to the annoyance of Mrs Coutts who thinks it totally unnecessary and doesn't mind telling them so.

In story-time, the three boys sit together on the carpet. Paul notices that Shane has plimsolls and Bobby, like himself, wears socks. They listen to their teacher, Miss Bishop, read fairy tales, one of them about a gingerbread man, their new-found friendship momentarily forgotten amongst the jostling of fifteen children. On the turn of each new page, a surge of panic to view the illustrations threatens to knock Miss Bishop backwards off her stool. She tries to calm the rush by facing the pages outward and revealing the images in a sweeping arc. Without seeing the pictures the words of the story are lost on Paul.

Lunch follows in the main hall. Meat, gravy, potatoes and peas. There's pudding too. Paul has never tasted chocolate sponge with green minty custard, and it is the highlight of his day. Paul passes by Carole as she stands in line waiting to enter the dining hall. Unable to contain his joy, he rushes over just to inform her about the green custard. Excited ripples travel down the line: green custard seems to be a firm favourite of almost everyone. Lunch also comes with an extended playtime, which makes Paul adore school dinners that much more.

The next lesson after lunch is PE, physical education. The changing room, consisting of two benches, two rows of hooks and two foot baths, is shared by both boys and girls. Undressing on opposite sides of the room, the boys are much quicker to ready themselves. Those without plimsolls walk in bare feet because wearing socks on the parquet flooring is slippy. Bobby and

Paul slap the floor with each footfall as they walk; Shane is told to put his pumps back on. In a dining hall cleared of tables and chairs, the children sit in a circle and roll a ball across the centre to a child opposite. The girls monopolise the fun by choosing to pass the ball only between themselves. Bobby intercepts a pass but doesn't roll it to Paul or Shane as they are sitting either side of him. Instead he rolls it over to a boy called Anthony, who sends it straight back into the open arms of a girl. Completely missing the educational part of this physical activity.

Class resumes shortly afterwards with threading counting beads on coloured strings and poking laces through the eyelets of various items of footwear depicted on pieces of card. By way of tying their own shoelaces, the able children and those with slip-on shoes no longer require assistance at break times. This independence rewards them with extra minutes of play, something Paul is quick to observe. It pushes him to try harder. The first 'cross over, tuck under and through' part is easy compared to the confusing looping bit. Though he struggles, Paul is no more than three lessons away from achieving this.

A few students are chosen at intervals to gather around the water table. As an exercise in buoyancy, children have to indicate which items they think will float to the surface and which will sink to the bottom. Paul excels and receives a red star to place on a wall chart alongside his name.

The final playtime break arrives. To the untrained eye it seems to be much the same as the morning one, twenty minutes of screaming, shouting and dashing about. Although from the perspective of Ms Lammers, a teacher who is a rather flowery soul who endorses peace and love, the playground is much less chaotic towards the end of the school day. Young active minds eventually begin to tire, meaning less whistle blowing, coffee spilling and yelling.

Since his arrival that morning, Paul has been waiting to be let loose on the toys. Miss Bishop says that *constructive play*, which means sharing and playing quietly, will follow drawing and colouring. Paul hastily scrawls a scribble using a dark blue crayon and urgently announces he's finished before most children have chosen which colour to use. Miss Bishop is having none of it and tells him if he's finished to sit quietly and wait, or if he prefers to lay down on the carpet. Paul falls asleep and isn't woken until home time.

Excluding the afternoon nap, this school routine soon becomes the norm. Every morning one child gets to change the icons on the weather board and another the numbers on the calendar. As soon as Miss Bishops asks, "Who wants—" a chorus of "Me" rings out.

At home Paul has to scramble to be noticed, and although the persistently annoying younger brother is becoming quite nimble when it comes to grabbing a share of the attention, any small advantage he previously utilised becomes invalid in this mixed class of big, middle and little siblings. To Paul it seems he has to wait ages before his pleas to be chosen are heard. All the children cry out to become the milk monitor, which means presiding over the crate of milk delivered each day by the aptly named Mr Moody. The school caretaker, in spite of his deeply weathered brow and crotchety scowl, is not at all grumpy, just busy. One lucky child will hand out the bottles and a second, the drinking straws. Paul, who is normally a terrible queuer, prefers the class to line up in an orderly fashion when he is monitor.

Paul's all-time favourite perk, due to the fact he gets to leave the classroom twice, both times unattended, is visiting the kitchen. Along the corridor he passes the staffroom. The lingering aroma of black coffee entices him to stop skidding. He slows to a dawdle, filling his nostrils before moving on. The cook writes down details of the day's luncheon, which are taken back to class for the teachers to choose their meal. Back he goes in his socks, skating across the wooden floor, slowing for a quick whiff of coffee before delivering their mealtime orders.

Unlike his first day, earning further stars for the wall chart doesn't come easy. Paul is currently in last place equal with four other children. In his first six weeks he has gained five stars in all. One red, two blue, a yellow and a green, ordinary colours worthy of a single merit point. The highly coveted gold and silver stars, awarded for outstanding achievements, are worth three times that. However, those stars elude him. Given to encourage, Paul is disheartened every time he counts those earned by the likes of Sarah Goody Two-shoes and the other more able students. Having competitive siblings has taught Paul to recognise the futility of striving for inaccessible prizes so he quits reaching for the stars.

Some children are predisposed to daydreaming and Paul is shaping up to be a master fantasist. He sees Miss Bishop as a beautiful princess. Her kind gaze and softly spoken narration captivates the attentive listeners whenever she sits down to read. The children are encouraged to lie back and allow her melodic words to evoke images of forests, giants and trolls. Paul harvests hope and contentment from the fables she recites. Whilst most children continue to scramble to see the pictures on the page, he lays back imagining. He easily drifts into the realm of make-believe, which wavers on the border of slumber. Developing a habit of comparing his possessions with those around him, Paul is satisfied that *his* teacher, Miss Bishop, is nicer than any other teacher in any other class.

Every playtime Paul attaches himself to Bobby and Shane, who are now considered mates. Shane lives in the street at the top of Paul's road. At five years old he isn't permitted to play out the front. Bobby's house is miles away so Paul regards them both as solely his school-gang. Together they play Batman and Robin, cops and robbers, and have turf wars with the other boys whenever the grass has been freshly cut. In the playground they walk around with arms draped over each other's shoulders, chanting "Who wants a game of cops and robbers? Who wants a game of cops and robbers?" The chain extends as students wanting to play link on.

The three of them always choose to be the robbers. Together they are becoming a formidable team, usually in the centre of the crowd and the culprits of most mishaps. Bad boy reputations have preceded them, although not unwarranted, and they become the prime suspects whenever teachers lack proof. They all have big brothers who have trodden the same path. Brothers who have shared their experiences and imparted knowledge in a manner of all kinds of naughtiness. It is all innocent, infantile behaviour which is sure to progress with a little imagination and some practice. Like crawling beneath the sandpit cover for secret gang meetings, or unscrewing the hard plastic knobs from the coat hooks and bouncing them, rather dangerously, around the cloakroom. A tip from his brother, Paul can't wait to place a crayon on top of a radiator to see it melt.

Paul's initial introduction to Yellow Class finishes at the end of July. Now that he can count well he knows exactly how many school years he has to complete before he can stay at home all day, like his dad. Two more years in the infants, four in the junior classes and five in senior school. Eleven more Christmases, which seems like a yawn-stretched lifetime and a half.

When he returns to school in September his class no longer occupies the carpet. They sit behind desks, are given pencils and told not to slouch. Miss Bishop greets the children and introduces Miss Young, a new classroom assistant. Furthermore she announces that Mrs Coutts has emigrated to New Zealand and, as a newly-qualified teacher, she will educate the upper students of Yellow Class. The students cheer when they hear this news. Over the summer holidays Miss Bishop had got married. She informs the children that they should now address her as Mrs Harris. Most of the class seem pleased with her happy news. Paul is less enthusiastic. Resenting the man who laid claim to *his* Miss Bishop, he senses loss, not joy. Barren, like the story-time carpet which will remain void of toddlers until a new influx arrives later in the year.

Paul's awkward, tatty-round-the-edges appearance and his irrepressible urge to fool about is quickly establishing him as the class misfit. His wayward actions have previously kept him in at playtime. Twice he has been scolded by Mr Graham, the headmaster. He and Shane had been given the privileged task of sorting and stacking the empty cartons: cereal boxes and plastic containers used when making models or creating collages. Behind the closed storeroom door, they concocted a witch's brew of cornflake crumbs, soap powder and washing-up liquid. With a stiffened paintbrush they mixed it up in their cauldron, a margarine tub. Then they ripped up strips of cardboard and pulled off the hardened drips blocking the nozzle of a glue bottle, adding a few squirts for good measure. Hovering before his pursed lips, Shane was building himself up to test the potency of its magical properties. Miss Young interrupted them. She discovered them trampling on top of brand new sheets of construction paper which had fallen from the shelves. Mrs Harris was livid and ordered them to the headmaster's office. Much like the giant from Jack and the Beanstalk, Mr Graham's booming voice rumbled loudly. It loosened Shane's bottom lip, which quivered as he sniffled. Paul, who is often a little slow to react, didn't cry. Just like the time Mr Graham slapped the back of his legs. Paul had been caught throwing wet paper towels at the skylight in the boy's toilet.

Paul didn't always get found out. One lunchtime he placed a drawing pin on a dining room chair. Ms Lammers, the warm, pleasant, laid-back teacher from Class Five, sat on it. She sprang up with a loud yowl. She was absolutely furious and screamed at those nearest, wanting to know who had done such a dastardly deed. Paul, Bobby and Shane sat two tables away, chuckling. The blame must have fallen elsewhere because it never found Paul.

Food at home is bland and Paul eats basically the same meals every day. For breakfast, Weetabix with watered-down evaporated milk that comes from a can. Or tap water when they run out. Worse than Weetabix is Wheat-A-Flakes, which would be self-explanatory if only they were called Wheat-A-Crumbs. These come in a large plastic sack and are way cheaper than any other cereal, bar porridge oats. Sharp particles of wheat husks sometimes become lodged in the crevices at the side of Paul's tongue and it also gives him indigestion. Paul normally has to vomit to relieve the acid burn. After school it is always bread and jam for tea. Strawberry when times are good, mixed fruit if money is tight.

Sunday, when the whole street smells of roasted meats and boiled vegetables, the family eat like kings. Steak and kidney pie out of a can, with mashed potatoes, tinned vegetables and gravy. Occasionally there is also a pudding of pear halves served with a splash of evaporated milk. However, it is the free school dinners that constitute Paul's main source of nourishment and his father encourages them all to stock up whilst at school.

Sometimes, when hunger impatiently paces back and forth, Paul can hardly contain his drool. The lunchtime preparations that waft down the corridor and drift beneath the classroom door are too much to bear. Not unlike the luscious, dark burgundy shine on the outer casing of the bean Paul is supposed to glue onto his collage. He munches and swallows it. Then he throws up all over the desk. He spends most of the morning lying down in the office of the nit-nurse, the smell of antiseptic lotions masking any bean-roasted aromas that lurk outside the door. It doesn't take him long to recover and by lunchtime he is at the serving hatch asking the dinner ladies for double helpings of mashed potatoes. Unfortunately, telling real potatoes from powdered is impossible at a glance. Powdered spuds make Paul heave: he really can't stomach them. Another thing he has to be weary of is roasted turnips. Which look like, feel like, though taste nothing like, roast potatoes.

At St Jude's waste is not permitted. So, under brotherly instruction, he tells a little white lie to the canteen staff who stand guard over the slop bucket. Fibbing that someone has sneezed over his plate, or, if the meat is too gristly, that it has been on the floor. But that is rare: most forkfuls bypass both tongue and teeth to enter his stomach at record speed. He is even prepared, providing it isn't Goulash, to sacrifice some of his playtime. Waiting until all the students have been served then returning to the hatch to request a second helping.

Chapter Five: Moving To Number Forty-six

Paul's family are soon to move house. Twenty-two is due to be demolished to make way for some lock-up garages as part of the council's modernisation programme for the street. The three eldest have already discovered the empty house at the bottom of the cul-de-sac. Fragments regarding their secret rainproof hideout reaches Paul's ears. Flitting behind the garden walls and gateways, he manages to follow them without detection, all the way to the bottom of the road.

Against the wall at the side of the property, a plank of wood leans at a slant below an open window. Hollow echoes of footfalls and his brothers' talking bounce through the opening. Determined to spy on them, Paul attempts to scramble up the precariously balanced slide. His feet are barely able to find a grip on the moist, blackened sheen covering its surface. After much effort Paul manages to grab hold of the windowsill. Hanging on by his elbows he pants, lacking the strength to haul himself up over the threshold. Paul refuses to surrender his midway accomplishment. He rests a while, hoping to muster up the power for one final lunge. The scraping of the shifting wood gives no forewarning before dropping away beneath his feet. Paul's chin suddenly hits the sill and his teeth chomp his tongue. The rough exterior wall scratches a layer from his knees. He cries out in pain. Determined not to relinquish his grip he defies the grazing sting and clings on.

Alerted by the commotion, Darren's head appears around a doorframe.

"Stop following!" he sternly commands.

Whingeing in a fat-tongued voice, Paul announces, "I'm stuck..."

"Go home," Darren orders.

"Right then, I'm telling Dad." Paul has learnt that sometimes this threat gets results.

"Tell him," Darren gambles, knowing full well that telling tales often backfires.

"Ok then, I'll tell Bill." As an ultimatum Paul issues this warning.

Bill, their lodger, is a roughneck twenty-year-old with shoulder-length ginger hair and a blackening canine tooth. His pale, freckly arms are scarred and adorned with homemade tattoos: three stars and a swastika. He is a teenage yobbo who has been thrown out of his home and done time in prison for fighting. As payment for their father's kindness in letting him stay, he's taken it upon himself to inject some additional order into the rowdy household. Becoming a second parent. He threatens and bosses them about as if he were a prison screw. Nobody likes Bill because he is a bully. Despite voicing threats, no one tells tales to Bill, their one common enemy. In fact, telling tales, even to their dad, often results in receiving a smack for blabbing. Hence Darren's risk in "Tell him."

Paul's taste buds detect a slight metallic tang. He cries out, "I'm bleeding," in a pathetic bid to provoke sympathy. Darren relents and hoists him up into the opening.

Paul, entering via the kitchen window, jumps down from the sink. Leaving behind the daylight he steps into the gloom of another room. Wooden panels cover all the downstairs windows. Paul's nostrils make up the shortfall of his vision. An overpowering stench, radiating from a corner of what is the dining room, claws at his sinuses. A sliver of daylight from the boarded window exposes a black cat, stiff, arched like the moon, lying dead on the floor. The lifeless creature riddled with maggots provokes sadness in Paul. An urge to comfort it with a stroke is deflected by the deathly stare coming from its final gaze.

At five and three quarters, emotions such as sympathy are still emerging, undeveloped, and these moments are fleeting. Paul rushes off to investigate the house. In the hallway he spies a lightbulb dangling from the ceiling. He climbs to the second stair and flicks the switch to illuminate the space. The walls, stripped bare, reveal the stubborn shards of bygone wallpaper and erratic red crayon scribbles. Astonished by this illuminating revelation, Darren calls up the stairwell, "The lecky's on!" Jason and Mark, who were lifting loose floorboards in their search of hidden valuables, bound on down the stairs. Darren then locates the coin-fed electricity meter and there, in amongst the dust and wires, he spies a ten pence piece. He quickly reaches for it but, with lightning speed, jerks back his hand. An exposed section of the mains wire kissed his finger. Besides the surprising jolt, Darren barely flinches and is soon flipping the coin up in the air to show off his fortuitous find. He feeds the coin through the meter, catching it as it falls out the bottom where the cashbox once was. Clocking up credit, he does this numerous times.

The three eldest then chat about gang rules and sharing, and squabble in a debate about forthcoming purchases. Trying to ascertain which lasts longer, bubble-gum flavour or rock-hard gob-stoppers. Expecting nothing, as he is not a member of their gang, Paul continues to explore.

On the first floor landing a small safe has been built into the wall, disguised behind matching wallpaper yet clearly visible due to slits around the edges and the keyhole. It is locked and the key sits in Mark's pocket. Naturally, it was empty when discovered but now it contains a large screwdriver and a glass cutter. The place smells much better upstairs, a typical empty house aroma of damp, dust, wood and plaster. Paul has no idea as he looks through the window that this room will soon become his bedroom. In a garden directly opposite a girl with masses of frizzy hair plays beneath an apple tree. He ducks down out of sight so she doesn't see him.

Four weeks later Paul bids farewell to the lamppost outside number twenty-two. It is a noisy affair moving to their new semi-detached home at number forty-six. Using two rather rattly supermarket trolleys, the family roll all their possessions down to the circle at the bottom of the road. Everything from stained mattresses, ripped settees to not-so-white kitchen goods are transported in this manner.

A chaotic din marks their arrival. Resident curtain-twitchers are drawn to their windows to witness the pandemonium. As orders are barked up and down the road, split boxes spew clothes over the pavement. Blackie and Podge trot back and forth carrying cans of dog food and other drool-proof items. It is tiring work for the children yet it is all done with great enthusiasm and relative speed. Last to go is the remaining piano, the other have been given away. The second, neither in nor out, stands wedged between the frame of the front door. It attracts a lot of attention in the days it remains there. A Caribbean, woman unable to resist, more than once tinkles the ivories treating those within earshot to a rendition of *Amazing Grace* and some lesser known ditties. Succumbing to the desires of the rag-and-bone man and the guy yelling "Any old iron," the instrument is eventually stripped bare.

Number forty-six, the last house on the left, has a small patch of uncut grass out front. A wedge-shaped grassy incline interrupted by two solid manhole covers. One has an indentation at the centre, which Paul discovers is ideal for playing marbles.

At the side of the house is a high, panelled fence with a gateway which opens into an enormous sunken garden. This is also wedge-shaped with a slope. A retaining red-brick wall runs along the length of the building, separating the higher and lower ground levels. The house appears to be set on top of a pedestal. A coal bunker and a low chain-link fence draw a thin line between this and the neighbouring plot. A brief interruption to the tall view-snatching panelling that surrounds the rest of the back yard. The dissuasive pungency of its damp creosote indicates its newness. At the furthest corner of Paul's new domain, through a jungle of brambles and overgrown weeds, hangs a second gate, which opens into a back alleyway. A concrete labyrinth of locked gates. A short-cut to the local park and shops.

Opposite the back door seven steps unite the split levels. The top stair, different from the rest, is awkwardly taller and not so rounded. Paul is destined to become intimately acquainted with this emotion-rending top step. His soon-to-become contemplation spot. Initially Paul curses the clumsy-sized step when he stumbles and bashes his shin. Blaming it for tripping him up, he slams his hand hard on the surface and then kicks it for making his hand sting. Later he growls in frustration at forgetting once again, annoyed about knocking away the protective crust of a large scab that was ripe for the picking. However, once the rhythm of his stride is firmly scored into his subconscious he bounds up and down them without incident, laughing at how he has finally outsmarted the stupid steps.

Despite all the stomping, slapping and insults, the mild-mannered, misunderstood step calmly listens and becomes a comfort. Paul chooses this spot to be bored. It is where he complains about a world where nothing good ever happens. The place he comes to weep and rant, to daydream about how things might have been and sulk about how things are. Although Carole and his father do, the three eldest hardly bother to use the steps. They are able to jump clear of the nettles that lurk over the edge of the surrounding wall in the shortest of short-cuts hardly worth the risk. But, to avoid a little brother who is apt to follow, it is always taken.

Shortly after moving in, Paul is sent to the shops to buy cigarettes for his dad. "Ten Number Six Tipped." He repeats the words over and over all the way there. In his tightly clenched fist he holds three coins: a two-bob piece, a shilling and tuppence. Paul's dad refers to the coins, in old pre-decimal terms. With conviction he uses the zebra-crossing to cross the main road and, as instructed, speaks to no strangers and gets into no cars. As the old shopkeeper hands him the packet he asks for seventeen and a half pence. Paul tells him he is wrong, that ten Number Six Tipped cost seventeen pence. The old man patiently explains that "All the fags have gone up half a pence," but as the man knows Paul's father he lets him off, though he won't be making a habit of it. Thus allowing him to complete his first shopping mission.

Directly outside the store, tickled by the way Paul hasn't once looked back over his shoulder, a proud father congratulates Paul. It has been a test which Paul has passed. His reward is some kali, a sherbet fountain of white lemony powder with a stick of liquorice to dip and lick. Unaccustomed to selecting sweets, this is not the best choice and Paul quickly learns he doesn't much care for the bitterness of liquorice. Fortunately this achievement is further rewarded with a little more freedom. In September, when Paul starts Green Class, he is allowed to walk to school unaccompanied by his dad. Instead Carole and Darren deliver him safely into the infant's playground.

Chapter Six: Green Class

Shortly after bashing the noses of the students who were tormenting him, Paul is summoned to the classroom and, despite any protestations about who said what, he receives an ear bashing from his teacher, Mrs Davies. He has to spend the remainder of his playtime, indoors with his mates, Bobby and Shane.

Mrs Davies, unlike Paul's last teacher, is a no-nonsense sort of a woman. Her strict, curt manner has the ability to provoke fear and command respect. Her shrill voice can silence the entire class with a strong shush or a powerful blast of "SIT DOWN!" Paul often experiences the wrath of Mrs Davies' impatience. She has the annoying knack of spotting who isn't paying attention then startling them with a loud slap on the desk. Paul's mind-drifts and dozes are often disrupted via a dusty blackboard rubber hurled with precision from across the room. Paul has quickly discovered that chalk dust is much easier to pat away from his jumper than it is from his trousers. He has a growing awareness of his own appearance and hates the way chalk, which is white, makes the dark fabric of his clothes look grubby and unwashed. Rejection from pupils who recoil with disgust and call him a tramp are also not easy to brush away. Regardless of the rhyme taught to him by his father, the scars from sticks and stones are merely scratches in comparison to those scored with hurtful words. He wants to retaliate, to lash out, but he isn't allowed to hit girls, only boys.

He's seen a real tramp. His dad pointed one out to him through a top deck window on the bus. Though it was sunny, the bearded old man wore coat upon coat and resembled a dreadlocked Womble (a litter-picking character from a children's TV programme). Famous about town, the tramp made his home on a traffic island amongst some trees. His name was Józef although most people called him Fred. Paul looks nothing like Fred.

Often a victim of his irrepressible emotions, when Paul is cheerful he babbles quite a lot. His babbles provoke anger. Anger means chastisement. Chastisement, tears or in the very least, sadness. Then Paul sulks and broods in silence for a while. In no time at all, a new wave washes over him. He forgets his gripe and, as bright speckles begin to re-emerge, so does his happy chatter. Green Class isn't conducive to jabbering. Lessons have progressively become more difficult and varied. Paul struggles.

When lessons restart after break, the children are instructed to take out their reading books. Everyone has completed red library books one, two and three in the *Through the Rainbow* sequence. Most have finished the yellow and blue series too. Some of the brightest students are close to finishing green book three. Paul is falling behind. However, unlike the star chart in his previous class, he is not yet disheartened with this measure of his ability. He is determined to complete orange book two. Concentration is the key to achieving this goal, yet once the children settle, silence and a lack of stimulus brings Paul's eyelids to rest and his head to flop forward. Around Jupiter table the children's silence is that little more quiet as they eagerly wait for Mrs Davies to slap the table. A thunderclap later, Paul is woken to her displeasure and also the conspiracy of those who share his table.

He spent midnight shivering on the landing, made to stand outside his bedroom door because he'd wet the bed, again. Paul would never voice this as a legitimate explanation for his tiredness. Darren also wets the bed, so it is quite normal for Paul to wake up wet numerous times a week. Avoiding the blame, Darren cleverly turns his undies around to make out Paul is the culprit. Sleep rarely comes easy. If it isn't the cold touch of a rubber mat beneath an ill-fitting sheet, or the sharp scratches from broken mattress springs sticking through a hole, it is the fear of monsters and shadows on the wall that keep him alert. Even though Paul knows the ghostly figure behind the door is only a dressing gown, it does nothing to halt his vivid imagination. Fixed with a fearful stare, blurry vision convinces him time and again he has seen the outline waver. Darren, whether snoring or not, is stirred with a nudge and a whispered question. Has he witnessed the same? Simply hearing Darren's frustrated response of "Go to sleep" is often enough to quell Paul's fear. When it isn't, Darren reminds him of the gun under the bed. Darren and Paul have successfully used this fictitious weapon to ward off imaginary creatures many times before.

Paul still very much believes in ghouls and monsters. Ages ago in number twenty-two when Darren, Carole and Paul all shared the same room, they were spooked by two square-headed figures silhouetted in the bedroom doorway. A claim they continue to uphold. Add to that a second incident, which occurred whilst they were hiding beneath the covers after hearing an eerie sound. Something at the bottom of the bed reached in and touched Paul's foot. This made him scream hysterically, a panic that made his dad leave his armchair and rush upstairs. The thing, perhaps interrupted by the landing light, fled without being seen.

Being the youngest in his family does tend to make Paul behave in a babyish way. It appears to happen automatically. With his peers he speaks much like they do, but whenever he is around older people, he tends to revert to his three-year-old, baby voice. He decides being in Green Class means he should grow up and start acting his age. He doesn't believe in the tooth fairy, not since leaving several teeth under his pillow and finding them still there the following morning. Plus he already knows exactly who Father Christmas is, yet despite this advancement his nighttime terrors and bed wetting continue to plague him. As part of his *growing up* he quits playing moms and dads, or in their case, moms and babbies. No more, when he craves a little mothering, does he wait, pleading in an infantile voice, for his sister to come dress him. Despite her bossy roughness, Carole makes for an adequate surrogate mother. With much regret he also severs his primary cord of affection, a goodnight peck on his dad's cheek. As fine as the thread may have been, numerous times since he has reconsidered this hasty decision. A fraying wish to retie that loose parental bond, one which weakens with each passing bedtime. Whilst he ponders, days crawl forward and the more certain he becomes that it's too late to go back. He constantly battles to act less wimpy, to remain true to this grown-up decision though in truth he hasn't much control over his spirit. Common sense conflicts with desires and daydreams clash with reality. Subliminal or instinctual, Paul continually yearns for the comfort of nurture. He gets a little of this via attention.

As Paul processes some of life's less sophisticated lessons, his classmates continue to read on through the rainbow. In Green Class there isn't a great deal of nurture to be had. In fact, it often seems purposely harsh. Every Monday morning, when the class register is taken, children hand over envelopes containing dinner money. This weekly ritual never changes and neither does Paul's home circumstances. Yet he must stand up, shout out "Free Dinners," and then sit back down. There is no hiding the fact Paul is poorer than everyone else. He regards this as the wrong type of attention.

When school trips come along, regardless of whether any lessons have been planned around them, Paul normally stays behind. One time, Lucy Pink handed Mrs Davies money to pay for his inclusion on a trip to a working farm. This was promptly returned to her parents under some pretext of charity being forbidden. Paul saw his dad break down in tears of frustration. He was livid, called it victimisation. Then Lucy's parents came around to the house and handed him the cash directly. On that trip Paul got to see cows, pigs, sheep and goats. He took a packed lunch of cheese sandwiches, a hard-boiled egg and a bottle of orange squash. Paul isn't keen on the cheap, low-calorie orange pop his family buys and thinks it smells like vomit. This, combined with engine fumes and the upholstery of the coach seats, made Paul queasy. Inevitably his weak stomach churned and he puked as soon as he stepped off the coach. Still, after relishing in the right kind of attention, namely sympathy, he received a chocolate Penguin bar from Lucy Pink and soon felt well enough to enjoy the rest of the day.

At six and a half, Paul's conscious world is expanding. His social development reaching a higher stage of awareness. He can now understand more than basic cartoon issues, simple emotions such as tears and laughter. He can see beyond his own worries and wants, and is able, to understand the feelings of others. Capable of expressing sympathy and compassion, this blossoming of his inner senses stretches out along the pavement on his walk to school. Unable to simply pass by the drying-out worms, he swoops to rescue them, placing them safely upon softer ground.

Therefore, witnessing his father's aggrieved reaction regarding the school trip and hearing words such as *being picked on*, compounds a sense in Paul that he comes from a family of misfits. He becomes increasingly self-conscious as he notices the differences between the haves and have-nots. Whilst Paul scrunches up his toes to hide the holes in his socks, his classmates swing feet wearing black pumps. At playtime they eat sweets, which they share. Paul eats snot and fingernails. The coarse material of his duffle coat itches and his free school uniform doesn't stand up to the rigours of boisterous play so rips and frays. Still, on the up side, as the year turns, more children join in the Monday morning mantra of "Free Dinners," and, regardless of the hardships these families are going through, Paul is glad of the company.

Paul has his gang, the Anti-Creeps, so it isn't like he spends the entire day sulking alone. Anti-Creeps know how to have fun for they are the adventurous kind. They have a covert communications system within Green Class. The plug-hole in the classroom sink carries messages to whichever one of them is brave enough to enter the girls' toilets and chat back through a wash basin in there. Lucy Pink and her friends also join in the conversations, asking if they *may* go to the toilet whenever paintbrushes are being washed.

In one area of the playground is an aviary housing budgies. Paul's brother Darren and his mates have the responsibility of feeding and cleaning. Every now and again, when lunch is too yucky to wait for seconds, Paul gets to point out his important big brother to the onlookers in the infant's playground. This comes with a teensy amount of kudos which Paul revels in. He even stops to chat. Out of school Darren rarely spares him more than three syllables. Just enough to tell Paul to, "Go away!"

Chapter Seven: Bill, Their some-of-the-time Lodger

A mouse is running about the kitchen, causing a commotion. Paul, holding a broom-handle spear, stands poised. Darren, armed with its worn-bristle head, pulls on a large sack of potatoes. As slick as the trickles of grease down the side of their stove, the rodent scarpers across the floor. Shrieking, they toss their weapons and lunge themselves up onto the kitchen worktops. They glimpse the mouse entering a gap at the side of the cooker. Once their embellished hysterics simmer down, they descend, retrieve their weapons and return to the hunt. Paul uses the broom handle to poke the darkened space beneath the stove and out comes the mouse, once again flitting across the floor to take refuge behind the potato sack. Darren creates a barrier in front of the cooker using a row of saucepans.

"Block the hole, block the mouse-hole," he urges, referring to what they think to be the rodent's primary access point. A fist-sized gap in the corner where the sink unit fails to meet the edge of the adjoining cupboard. Paul backs himself into the corner, heels pressed tightly together to cut off the mouse's retreat. Darren shifts the sack of spuds. The mouse darts right, heads towards the pans then switches back towards Darren, who instantly backs off. It skirts along the wall, halting to rest in another corner before making a bold dash across the open floor towards Paul. Darren lobs the broom head with lightning speed and thundering power. It whacks Paul's ankle, making him jump and howl. In a split second the mouse makes quick its escape, vanishing through the unguarded hole. Despite the throbbing pain of a ripening bruise Paul is relieved the mouse got away. He forms a picture. Attentive offspring with twitching whiskers and ruffled fluff all listening to Papa Mouse retelling his courageous tale of escape.

Saucepans glide so well across the tiled surface of the kitchen floor. Darren and Paul invent a crashing game, one without rules. Just slide and collide. Scrape and bang, back and forth they send the pans. One of the handles breaks off just as their exasperated father enters to see who is making such an awful racket. Luckily Darren and Paul receive no thrashing, only a tongue-lashing before being sent to their room.

Within half an hour they are jumping up and down on the bed twirling underpants around their index fingers, singing "*Swing your knickers in the air, in the air...*" Bouncing about in circles having such a laugh. Whipping pants around and around, then flinging them at each other like wet rags. Bouncing, flinging, laughing on and on until Paul stops dead, wide-eyed and mouth agog. Darren jumps on, singing and swinging. Taking aim he enquires, "What's up with yuu...?" Words trailing off, he turns around to see Bill scowling. Paul dives beneath the covers. Darren is yanked by his elbow off the bed and shoved against the wall. Bill rips back the bedding, grabs Paul by the ankle and pulls him towards the edge of the bed. He turns his head towards Darren. "Don't you fuckin' move!" His aggression stops Darren in his tracks. After a rough bit of tugging and shoving the two are instructed to stand in silence. When Paul's tears subside he is left with crimson finger marks and Darren, a grazed shoulder. Their resentment of Bill rises to a new level.

It is a confusing relationship Paul has with Bill. Ensconced within the family, he has long been a feature in Paul's life. His heavy-handedness is viewed as a great help to their father and it is widely accepted that his orders are an extension of their dad's will. Bill's many contacts and dodgy dealings benefit the family, often keeping their heads afloat. Although sometimes a thug with a grudge may come pounding on the front door, and just like when the rent-man knocks, the children squash together behind the settee until the silhouette outside the window dissolves back into daylight. Whenever the police come calling, the children will, upon his command, tell lies. Though this is not entirely foolproof with Carole around. She once interrupted Mark's misleading response to the officer's enquiries with "You're telling lies, Dad told us not to tell lies." So on that instance Bill, who was concealed in the rafters of the roof, got taken away to be questioned over a brawl in the Beckley Tavern. They released him soon after.

On the one hand Paul sees Bill as a brute who is often drunk. A horrible tormentor, who enjoys frightening children. Watching *The Adventures of Black Beauty* one rainy Sunday around tea-time, Paul is locked in the grip of suspense, watching with bated breath as Albert enters the witch's garden to retrieve his kite. A flash glimpse of movement lurking around the edge of Paul's vision provokes a side glance which instantly becomes a face of terror.

A maniacal glare, eyelids turned inside out and a sinister grin. Bill's wet face pressed against the grey windowpane sends a terror shockwave straight through Paul, who gasps and bawls. Bill is always catching the children out in one way or the other. If they aren't sitting nicely watching the television, they're more than likely doing something that merits his chastisement. Then he'll bang on the window, point upwards and mouth the words, "You, bed, now!"

Often the one who inspects the housework before allowing the children to play out, Bill will rub his finger over the skirting boards and pelmets, searching for dirt. His dusty finger will then be wiped across a cheek or forehead with instructions to clean the room properly. He takes pleasure in secretly scrawling dates in the dust on the top of wardrobes and in other out-of-reach places, then revealing them some time later. Bill's presence, even when he lies snoring on the settee, creates tension. Yet whenever Paul is teased about not having a mother, he boasts that dads are way cooler than mums and that he has *two of 'em*. Furthermore, when making Christmas cards in class he addresses them to both Dad and Bill.

There are also hidden advantages to having a *Bill* living under the same roof. One night, disturbed by raised voices coming from the dining room, Carole leaves her bed and wanders downstairs. Her father and Bill are having a blazing argument. On the table a handwritten note sits next to a glass of water and a line of white tablets. Carole is immediately sent back to bed and the row quickly peters out. A couple of days later Carole, who knows better than to go rummaging around in her father's bedroom, is in there looking for nothing in particular. She finds fragments of a torn letter scattered in his wastepaper bin. Ever curious she retrieves the pieces, locks herself in the bathroom and begins jigsawing them together. Not the shiniest button in the box, Carole hasn't made any connection to the note in front of her and the fading images of a few nights before. It comes as a bit of a shock to see her own name mentioned in this note addressed to Mark. It reads, 'Dear Mark, sorry for what I have done, try to keep the kids together, and you'll have to explain it all to Carole, you know how thick she is. Dad xxxxx'. Regardless of the seriousness, any dire implications are somewhat overshadowed by his last line. Carole, perturbed at being called thick, returns the torn pieces and, without a word to anyone, banishes the memory to the cavernous recesses of her brain. Striking a discordant chord, the song and dance of everyday life plays on undeterred.

Bill, determined to instill a disciplined attitude, decides that the children need to be drilled. Darren and Paul think themselves fortunate to be called downstairs so soon after being caught flinging pants around. Being allowed to participate in what at first seems like a fun training programme with instructions to run around the block, a circuit of roughly one mile. At staggered intervals Bill blows on a whistle to send them off. Firstly Paul followed by Carole twenty seconds later. Darren jets away hot on their heels with Jason and finally Mark bringing up the rear. Bill pits the children against each other with the notion of punishment for any who lag or get overtaken. The race is on.

Paul sprints from the bottom of the cul-de-sac to the grove that leads into the triangular back park. Much to his frustration, as he proceeds through the play area and enters the adjoining housing estate, Carole, who is surprisingly swift on her feet, overtakes him. He passes by the alleyway that leads to his back garden and continues on to the garage area, which will eventually lead out onto the busy road near the shops. Carole has already vanished up ahead. Behind him Darren is making ground. He makes an exerted effort, only to be hindered by a searing pain below his ribs. Darren flies past him as he hits the main road. Paul's petulant response is to stamp and then slump onto his bottom on the floor. Darren doesn't stop and, lacking a proper audience, neither does Paul. Back on his feet he manages to hold off Jason and Mark, who are yet to come into sight.

The lengthy main road eventually turns into the street at the top of the cul-de-sac, the one his classmate Shane lives on. Paul manages to summon up an extra push now that the end is in sight. At the finish point Bill and Darren wait as Carole desperately encourages Paul to run faster. He glances behind to see Jason and Mark sprinting hard along the home straight. Head to head, gritting their teeth with more determination than a dog on a rag. Bill's provocative jeers cultivate sibling rivalries that need no encouragement. The losers, Jason and Paul, are given twenty press-ups.

In the weeks that follow nobody except Carole enjoys the running. Before long, the three eldest conspire to nip down the alleyway and climb over a fence leading to the main road. Resting, they time their arrival so nobody loses, except a baffled Paul, that is. He wonders at which point on the route they managed to pass by without him seeing them.

Typical of many fitness fads, this one doesn't last. Karate classes also flit by with a couple of visits. In the car park Jason becomes involved in a pushing tussle with one of the instructor's sons. Knocked off his feet, Jason runs home, intimidated by the boy's size and skill. Paul's dad, furious to learn that Jason hadn't even returned a single punch, escorts him straight back with Mark and Darren in tow.

"Is that him?"

Darren nods.

"Right, now go get him!" Spurred on by his father's command, Jason leaps into action, grabbing the culprit around the neck and punching him three times in the face. Darren, quick to respond, sets upon the brother who tries to intervene. Almost instantly, the point being made, Paul's dad calls out, "Ok! Stop now, that's enough."

Jason and Darren cease their attack and both boys back away, bringing an end to any future karate lessons and also their dad's *matter of principle*. His father's principles can often appear reactionary and excessive to Paul. The phrase *this will hurt me more than it will hurt you* sounding hollow at the point of receiving the cane. Yet the children largely accept that his instructions and punishments are issued out of love and for their own benefit. The same cannot be said for Bill.

Chapter Eight: A Day Trip To Blackpool

Windsor Park is a vast green area of playing fields within walking distance of Paul's house. Many football pitches fit into the park. It also hosts a recreational playground consisting of six big kids' swings and two baby ones. Well equipped, it has a longer than usual slide, a see-saw and a fair-sized climbing frame. There is also a rocket-shaped bench thing that rocks back and forth in a juddery motion. Skirting one of the bordering edges, a small brook flows, making this park Paul's favourite. In the school summer holidays a visiting council-run group organises play activities for local children. By submitting a small deposit of a sweater or any other item of clothing, children are allowed to borrow sports equipment and toys. They can obtain all manner of playthings: brightly-coloured hula-hoops, long-legged wooden stilts, springy metal pogo-sticks, skittles made of plastic, and a selection of bats, balls and rackets.

When at a loose end, Paul and his siblings often attend and generally behave themselves. The play scheme, as the children call it, arrange a sponsored walk which takes place towards the end of the school holidays. Every child that takes part, no matter how much money they raise, is eligible for a seat on the coach. A coach that takes them out on a day trip to Blackpool. Making up for the materialistic shortcomings at home, their father often grants a little more freedom. This comes mostly in the form of playing out unsupervised and allowing them to travel much further afield. As there are no additional costs to the family, excluding money for fairground rides and sweets, he signs their permission slips which are then exchanged for sponsor forms.

Carole and Paul go knocking on stranger's doors, asking to be sponsored. Generally receptive to their charming requests people scribble varying commitments like offering two pence for every mile they cover, or paying ten pence overall, regardless of how much they walk. The spaces on the forms are filled quickly. Jason adds up his forthcoming earnings and decides it would be prudent to request a second sheet. By telling the organisers he has lost his initial form, he obtains a replacement. Later submitting to them the form with fewest sponsors, he cashes in on people's goodwill by keeping the money.

One circuit around the top section of the park constitutes a mile, give or take, and the sponsored walkers stroll around it for most of the day. Paul manages five turns, earning a total two pounds and ten pence. Carole manages six circuits and nets two pounds fifty-two. Paul's brothers appear to be jogging, which seems to be allowed. Their substantial proceeds are much appreciated and received without question. All the children qualify for the free trip to Blackpool.

On the journey, the three eldest sit at the back of the coach, Carole and Paul at the front. Their dad remains at home. A youth worker gives Paul a magic pill to stop him being travel sick, and despite the noxious smell of upholstered seats and engine fumes, it works. Without incident they arrive at their destination with a packed lunch of cheese sandwiches, a bottle of orange squash and a hard-boiled egg. Instructions are issued to be back at the coach by six-thirty and the three eldest vanish.

Chaperoned by two of the youth workers, Carole, Paul and a small group of children head in the direction of the Tower. Passing by the sweet smelling purveyors of Blackpool rock and sugar-dummies, Paul hankers after a walking-stick full of smarties. Carole points upwards at a Kiss-Me-Quick cowgirl hat hanging from a top shelf. The shopkeeper asks her if she would like one. She says yes and the man unhooks it using a bamboo pole. She beams as he places it on her head. A misunderstanding, the hat is swiftly snatched away after one of the youth workers informs the vendor that she doesn't have any money. Carole's smile does a one-eighty and Paul's belly grumbles in protest as they continue on past all the candied delights.

The tide is way out, and although the Irish Sea appears to be miles away, its bracing breeze brings a rusty, sprout-like aroma to waft into the gaps around their collars. A musky smell of darkened seawater, sugar and chip shops fuses to create a nasal imprint that will linger long after the trip. They walk across the damp sand, avoiding the expanse of rippling puddles being hit by the rushing winds. Some of the children delight in kicking up splashes which they aim at the youth workers. Further along Carole and Paul watch as the children rush over to an old man offering donkey rides for a small fee. The man holds the reins as he leads two of his customers down the beach at a slow walking pace. Paul recalls riding on a white horse. A previous girlfriend of Bill's had ridden her horse into the street one summer. It made such an impression, neighing, snorting and loudly clip-clopping. The beast was frighteningly huge and warnings about being kicked were issued whenever a child stepped behind it. With a bunk up from Bill, she hoisted Paul onto the saddle and they rode from number twenty-two to the bottom of the cul-de-sac and back again. A distant memory that seems like a dream.

Once all the children have ridden, the gap-toothed old man with smiley eyes offers Carole and Paul a free jaunt across the sand. They sit together, Paul in front, the cold momentarily banished. The donkey walks languidly, which suits Paul who savours the moment. Although a little afraid he manages a couple of strokes of the donkey's mane. The hair is not at all fluffy but tough and coarse.

They do a lot of walking around. Looking but not touching is the order of the day, especially inside the amusement arcade. The bright lights and electronic noises, a chaotic cacophony of sound and vision, entice the wide-eyed child. Too tempting not to nudge the teetering piles of two-pence pieces that hang over the ledges of the coin push machine. Checking all the return-slots, any coins found are soon lost in the hope of gaining more. Carole spots Jason milling around the entrance of the arcade, and he asks them if they have seen Darren and Mark. They haven't. He tells Paul he knows how they can get a free ride on one of the fairground attractions. So Paul leaves the group and follows Jason. They sneak up the exit ramp of the train ride, and when the ticket collector is preoccupied they rush from cover and, undetected, take one of the empty seats. There's a mechanical tapping and the train pulls out of the station. Excited that they have gotten away with it, Paul relaxes and watches the carriage slowly climb and climb and climb.

It is awfully high, so high he can see the beach, the sea and, way off in the distance, the Tower. Unexpectedly the train reaches the end of the track. Nothing ahead of them except thin air and grey sky. Then whoosh, Paul's stomach hits the back of his throat as the bench he is sitting on falls away beneath him. Plummeting downwards the sheer horror of his plight sends Paul into hysterics. Screaming, tears streaming, his knuckles whiten as he clings on to a safety bar that does nothing to secure him in his seat. Slipping backwards then sliding forwards he cries to be let off. Jason appears unfazed but Paul cannot see that through his own traumatic yells of *Make it stop, make it stop*. At one point, as his hands become weak through over-squeezing, he seems to be held in his seat by nothing but his gritted teeth and clenched chin. A snivelling wreck exits the big dipper. Jason, who wants to go again, laughs calling Paul a *big babby* after he declines his offer of another ride.

They eventually catch up with Darren and Mark when boarding the coach home. Earlier in the day Jason had scarpered, leaving the two of them in the firm clutches of an irate arcade attendant. He caught them red-handed attempting to fish trinkets and soft toys out of the mechanical crane game. Inserting their hands up the deposit slot, they had managed to grab some items whilst trying to reach for a packet of cigarettes with a pound note stuck to it. They were locked in a security office and missed out on much of the day. The police were called but no charges were pressed. Instead they were banned from the arcade with a strong ticking off.

Paul is reunited with Carole sitting at the front of the coach. She is smiling and wearing a Kiss-Me-Quick hat. It takes quite a while for the coach to reach the motorway home. Firstly it joins a procession of crawling vehicles. Through panels of vibrating glass, sightseers point, their faces lit by the reflected colours. Blackpool illuminations, a thrilling climax for the accompanying adults. Paul is already falling asleep.

Chapter Nine: Winter

Always a pleasant way to begin his day, Paul wakes up dry. He slept soundly without the usual bladder-release-inducing dream of himself taking a long and somewhat refreshing wee, a recurrent theme that seems to occur more in the winter time. He pats the mattress to double check, and satisfied, he reaches over to Darren's side. That too is dry. Deep in the land of nod, Darren's protruding tongue, parched and pulsing, expressing the laboured breaths from his arid throat. The air about the room is cold enough to produce wisps of breath mist.

Paul snuggles back under the covers knowing in a short while his dad will begin calling the children to wake up. Stretching out his legs takes effort. Heavy coats, thick curtains and itchy blankets tucked tightly around him restrict his movements. Between the many layers, newspaper has been inserted and there's a slight rustling sound as he jiggles about. He folds back the hem of a curtain so the metal rings no longer chill his neck. His foot brushes the cold glass surface of a pop bottle resting near the bottom of the bed. An improvised hot-water bottle that had been filled the night before from a boiling kettle. It doesn't crack or leak from the heat. In fact, it does the job perfectly, or close to. Paul avoids touching it. At night it is usually scorching hot and by morning, freezing cold, so he nudges it over to Darren's side of the bed.

"Mark! Mark?" Paul's dad, who generally rises early, is calling from downstairs. Soon everyone will be up and about. Mark responds with a weak, sleepy "Yes."

"Are you up? Mark?" His dad receives a second, much clearer "Yes!" before he continues.

"Jason? Jason? Jason!"

"I'm up," Jason's response showing more annoyance than is probably wise.

For once Paul is glad to be the youngest. His dad always wakes the family in descending order, which, on cold mornings like this, rewards him with extra cosy time.

"Darren? Darren?" By now it would be fair to say everyone, including the neighbours, is awake, although not all are out of bed yet.

"Darren, are you up?" Darren responds in the affirmative.

"No, he's not," Paul adds.

"Darren, get up, now!"

Darren leaps out of bed, stomping heavily on the floor to demonstrate some kind of movement.

"I *am* up," he calls out, directing this look of irritation towards Paul. He then grabs at the covers, attempting to rip them from Paul's determined grasp.

Carole, who often pre-empts her dad's call, interjects, "I'm already up, I am, Dad."

"Me too." Paul lets loose his grip and springs out of bed before Darren can say any different.

There is never a mad rush for the bathroom. Even with Paul's growing awareness, personal hygiene is not a priority. In fact, it could be fair to say that unless instructed to wash, all but Carole will rub the sleep from their eyes and be satisfied they are ready for school. A fake, worn and cracked bar of soap, which appeared ever so realistic, was once placed in the bathroom soap dish. What initially started as a lighthearted prank soon became a contentious issue about telling lies. The three eldest had been ordered to go back upstairs with strict instructions that this time they were to wash behind their ears and to use soap. When all three returned a second time claiming they had washed properly, they got a proper scolding and weren't allowed out all day. Luckily, when Paul attempted to use the pink plastic forgery, he called down to his dad saying that he couldn't make any bubbles and was praised for his honesty.

The stone-cold hot water tap also has a habit of telling lies. It has been a very mild winter so far, however an unexpected cold snap has moved in overnight. Crystal fingers have clawed through a crack in the bathroom window. Icy globules covering the pane, adding a sense of frosted realism to the cloudy manufactured glass. This morning Paul doesn't wash. He descends the stairs. Grey and gloomy, the light through the window reveals a message scraped into the melting ice: *Paul wets the bed.* His teasing taunt, everyone has one. Mark is called *Spotty* due to the smattering of freckles that dons his face. Jason is ridiculed with gibes of *Runaway* after he'd spent an afternoon escaping life's hardships by running off. Darren suffers from patches of eczema behind his knees and is therefore teased with the name *Scabby*. Carole is just plain *Goofy* and so are her teeth. With their toughened training these insults are not meant to hurt when flung, although each child knows differently. Paul pushes the window slush around. Obscuring his name he replaces it with Darren.

The dining room is tropical. The fire is on full. In the kitchen all the gas rings are dancing and the oven door is flung open to allow the flames to heat up the place. Five minutes later, the light brown circle upon the kitchen ceiling deepens. Made previously, when Bill fell asleep on the sofa whilst running a bath, through a thumb-sized hole a glistening drip hangs. Paul is the first to notice the fall of water droplets. Conveniently splatting onto the draining board of the sink before flowing down the plughole. It makes a repetitive tap, tap, tap sound, one Paul instantly recognises. In a matter of ticks the taps become a trickle and soon accelerate into a continuous cascade. Paul alerts the whole family with a bellow and the children spring into action. Darren turns off the water by the main stop-tap beneath the sink, whilst Jason stands on the work surface holding a saucepan to catch all he can. Carole waits, ready to pass him an empty pan whilst Mark takes the filled ones which he empties into the sink. Paul's father instructs him to run upstairs to fill up the kettle before the pipes run dry. Sometimes, when temperatures below zero are forecast, the bath tub is pre-filled with fresh water in case of a burst pipe. On this occasion Paul's father was caught unawares. Without a mains supply the flow slows to a dribble then a drip. A tea towel placed on the draining board cushions the final few splashes. The floor is then mopped dry. Unfortunately, an eventful morning such as this doesn't merit a day off school. The children eat breakfast and leave home a little later than usual.

Over a crunchy layer of iced particles Carole and Paul trudge through the back garden and off up the alley. Darren has already bolted off in the hopes of catching up with a school mate. Mark and Jason, having further to travel, are also long gone. The two little ones skate across the estate towards the lock-up garages that lay just beyond, Paul incessantly scratching beneath the hood of his duffle coat.

"Om 'itchin', am yow?"

Carole doesn't respond with words, instead she pulls Paul's hood down and clasps his head in both her hands to inspect his hair. In a chimp-like fashion she picks a total of four head lice and twice as many strands from out of his crown.

Announcing, "You've got bugs," she pulls the hood back over his head as if to contain them.

"Yow must have gid 'em me," Paul accuses.

Carole is often blamed, without grounds, for bringing nits into the family.

"So how come I ay itching then?" she pronounces gleefully, "and stop scratchin'."

Chiding Paul, they continue on. Carole's last harsh remark comes out of concern. In playgrounds and the streets, there is a stigma attached to having bugs.

Veering off the main footpath Carole heads over to the corner of the garages to explore. Part of her routine is to look for abandoned infants on her way to school. There are a few places that Carole regularly inspects, like the small gap between the boundary fence and last garage. Convinced that one day she will find an unwanted baby, one that she can keep. They exit the garage and continue towards the main road via a passageway. Carole leans over a low wall to inspect the base of some box hedge bushes to her right and Paul does the same to his left. They see some scattered cigarettes, and frozen amongst the leaves and stuck fast to the ground a two-pence piece. After fingers fail him, Paul manages to prise it loose by kicking at it with the back of his heel.

They nip into Star's newsagents to buy some sweets. Half a penny can buy a small packet of Fizzers, ten tablet-sized sweets wrapped in clear plastic. They purchase four. Paul fights the urge to empty a whole roll straight into his mouth, but instead he makes like Carole and pretends he has taken a wonder pill to make him walk faster. With extra added energy, Paul zips off to skid down the icy slope leading to the children's library. He conceals himself beyond the entrance. Carole ambles unsteadily down the un-gritted footpath. When she nears the bottom Paul lunges out from his hiding place, and reaching for her arm with pincered fingers he chants, "Pinchfield, no returns."

Carole reacts, twisting her body quickly enough to avoid Paul's pinch.

"Ha ah, ya missed," she chuckles.

Paul, now on his backside, watches her awkwardly slip and shuffle away like an Arctic penguin. The thick hood of his coat is frosted after saving him and his lice from a severe head bump. He doesn't rush to give chase. Carole has already reached one of the game's designated safety zones, a signpost that reads Pinchfield Crescent. Anywhere else along the road and it is open season to give or receive a nasty nip in their walk-to-school game. In springtime or snow, this scenario, to varying degrees, is played out every time they walk this route. Carole decides to eat another energy pill before embarking on the hundred metre rush to seek sanctuary behind the second safety zone, another street sign at the far end of the Crescent. Lurking there, his friend nowhere in sight, Darren is waiting for them to catch up. Paul greedily scoffs the rest of his pep pills and skates straight by his sister. Carole's panting breath and beaming smile fizzles as she is left to dawdle precariously alone.

"What are you eating?" Darren questions with suspicion.

"Nothing... I've finished 'em now."

"Sweets? You coulda give me one." Darren reaches over and pinches Paul, adding an extra twist.

"Pinchfield... no returns," he speaks quickly before Paul can interject with a "returns" call.

"Ow, ya fuckin' bastard."

"Right, I'm telling Dad you swore."

"No I didn't... I said, fluffin' basket."

Darren gives Paul a nudge into a low hedgerow, quite a normal thing to do with this particular hedge on this particular journey. Instead of springing back off it, Paul finds himself falling through a gap. Icy wet leaves brushing his face and neck, his hands land in the front garden of someone who is banging angrily on the window.

"Get off my garden!" the old man yells through a now-open window. "I know which school you go to..."

"No, you don't," Paul challenges the claim.

"I'll be speaking with your headmaster," the man threatens.

As the two of them make their escape, Darren informs Paul that the old man does know which school they attend. Not only because their school is the only one in this particular edge of the town, but because the red of St Jude's uniform can be seen through an opening in Darren's coat.

It tries to snow. Fine icy crystals, the wrong kind of snow, flick and flurry in the gusting currents that blow around the nearby flats. The brothers stop to warm themselves. Vented from the basement of the high-rises, hot fragrant air is expelled through lint-clinging grids. Industrial dryers from the laundry room blow perfumed drafts onto the faces that compete for prime position. Carole catches up with her brothers here and joins in the fun of pushing, pulling and poking. Sending one another hurtling out into the chilly cyclones. Carole informs Darren about Paul's head lice. Removing his hood gives Paul a tactical advantage until Darren lets him know, under no uncertain terms, that *it's not funny*. They stay huddled there in the warmth for as long as they dare before braving the elements again.

By the time Paul reaches school his socks are sopping wet. His shoes, which were new last September, now possess twelve weeks' wear and tear. Small cubes of slush fill gaps in the worn-out heels, and the front of his right shoe is beginning to chomp at the ground like a hungry frog.

He squeezes a couple of drips out the end of his rumpled socks and places his shoes on the hot water pipes that run beneath the cloakroom benches. As he crosses the brown parquet flooring of the assembly hall, a trail of darkened streaks follow behind his footfalls. This seems to amuse the other children. Or perhaps they snicker at the curious toe poking through a hole in his sock. Giggling girls who shriek and back away didn't used to bother Paul, but now he sits cross-legged on the floor, indignation colouring his face. Gripping the scrunched end of his sock in-between his toes, he manages to obscure the hole.

As Mr Graham, the headmaster, addresses the assembled infants of Yellow, Blue and Green Classes, a policeman, PC Spoon, enters the hall. Paul shrinks low behind the row of children seated in front of him. His head itches, and as he battles to remain still, the itch is mirrored by one growing in his toes.

Chilblains again. Often dogged by these in the winter Paul recognises the onset of this fiery throbbing with dread and frustration. A condition caused by bad circulation and exposure to the cold. Chilblains make his toes redden, swell and crack. The itching often becomes intolerable, the pain so fierce that Paul has no qualms about submerging them in urine. Until then all he can do is rub and scratch.

Fortunately PC Spoon has come to give a talk about pedestrian awareness and not trespassing onto people's property whilst walking to school. He advocates the use of the *Green Cross Code*, a televised public-service campaign on how children should stop, look and listen before they cross the road. After a short speech a television set flickers on. Examples on how-to and how-not-to get to the other side of the pavement. Foolish children about to step out into oncoming traffic are stopped by the Green Cross Man who shows them the correct manner to cross a busy road. The film also shows children from various schools using the lollipop man. Then two dogs that sit at the zebra crossing: the clever dogs wait for the cars to brake before trotting across. The two dogs are Blackie and Podge. Paul can hardly believe that his pets are on telly. PC Spoon commends them for doing it correctly and Paul spends the rest of the day bragging about it. His boastful claims are backed up by a boy from another class, Martin Murphy, who lives in the same street at number thirty-six and recognises Paul's dogs.

The only upside Paul can think of to winter, apart from Christmas, is being greeted back home by a bowl of steaming hot soup. Whenever the temperatures drop, Paul's dad prepares a pan of soup and a stack of bread and marge ready for when the shivering children return home from school. Today it is mushroom soup, which is Paul's second favourite after oxtail. Following his tea, thanks to Carole's big gob Paul is subjected to a torturous lice extermination regime consisting of burning malt vinegar rubbed into his hair and a fine-toothed comb being scraped across his scalp. Red raw and sore and stinking like a bag of chips, Paul holds his stinging head over a sheet of newspaper and listens to the nits hit the page as his dad mercilessly yanks his head this way and that in his attempt to tackle Paul's knotted locks. In between the painful tugs and irritation Paul enjoys the intimacy of his father's full attention and feeling the warmth from his hands as he seeks out the pesky critters hiding behind his ears.

Chapter Ten: Christmas

In the final week of school before the festive season begins in earnest, St Jude's holds two Christmas parties. One for the students of the junior classes and another for the infants. As a nominal fee is required, Paul thinks it is highly unlikely that Darren, Carole and he will attend.

Echoes of, "We can't afford it," a well-worn phrase, reverberate at the thought of asking. A standard response made final by a firm reminder of "Because you haven't got a mom, that's why." The message has finally sunk in. The crumpled permission slip rests with the painted scraps of artwork that litter Paul's school drawer. He no longer pesters his dad with requests for payment, aware that his unemployed father has no money for all the added extras a family of five children requires.

He understands from past conversations that his dad couldn't hold down a job *and* take care of five children. That going out to work would mean the children would, most probably, be put into an orphanage. Paul's proposed solution for his father to marry a new mother is humorously dismissed with "I had enough with the first one and I won't be doing that again." And, true to his word, Paul's dad never entertains any ladies or goes out on any dates. There are no doting grandmothers to soften the hard edges of daily life. Or any aunties that pop by to lend a hand. Women hardly feature in Paul's household. Bill does, on occasion, entertain a new lady friend. Long-haired dolly birds that wear fur coats and exotic perfumes. Fleeting visits, their affectionate smiles, lip-sticked cigarette butts and trailing fragrance, leave Paul with a pleasant impression of what having a mother could be like. The absence of his real mother is the sole reason the family go without. Nevertheless, there is no wishing for her return. With no memories, conscious or otherwise, he doesn't pine for what he doesn't know. Instead he yearns for all the material things that money can buy.

When an unknown lady strolled through the back garden of the old house, toddler Paul threw up a quick glance then continued playing in the mud. Not that he actually remembers, it is just something he hears mentioned. How his mother came by one day but didn't stay. The only advantage Paul can see to being motherless is whenever he tells an old lady he doesn't have a mom, sympathetic gazes and sweets often follow.

***

Yuletide, a magical event full of miracles. A tide that temporarily washes away life's hardships in its yearly ebb and flow. So significant to him that he measures the passing of his childhood from one festive season to the next. Christmas gifts — Paul's reward for saying his prayers every night. Paul absolutely loathes Boxing Day. To the disappointed child who didn't receive an Etch-a-Sketch, counting the days till next Christmas seems to compound his frustration. Presently that wait is almost over, plus the fee to attend this year's school party has been waived and Paul lines up between Shane and Bobby, eager to enter the school dining hall. Under instruction to remain calm and quiet, the class troop along in single file.

Stretching the width of the hall, three rows of trestle tables, one for each class, have been laid out with coloured napkins and Christmas crackers, paper plates and plastic glasses. Interspersed all the way along the table's centre, resembling large coloured lightbulbs, glass jugs of orange squash and lemon cordial further brighten the merry scene. It is a weak façade, this calm. Hushed whispers soon bubble into boisterous babble about cake. Paul's stomach groans and his mouth waters at the thought of it. Greedy eyes bulge in search of delights not yet placed on the tables. Paul can hardly contain himself. Breaking ranks, some children surge forward, resulting in a melee to secure places next to specific friends. Bobby, Shane and Paul sit next to one another.

A parade of jolly dinner-ladies, festively bedecked with tinsel bowers and themed aprons, convey plate after plate of party foods. Delivering their array of delectable delights, the remaining surface of the table is soon covered. Mini-sausages skewered on cocktail-sticks in one hand and chunks of pineapple with cheese in the other. Bowls of salted crisps and trays of sausage rolls. The flow continues. They proceed to lay down various platters of sandwiches: egg and cress, meat paste, boiled ham and cheddar cheese. The ravenous kids begin to fidget, Paul more than most. Lastly, but by no means least, the cupcakes arrive. Sponge fancies in paper cases decorated with ivory icing and multi-coloured sprinkles, diamond sugared jellies and chocolate drop smarties. Barring the watercress and potato crisps there's not a vegetable in sight.

With napkins spread across on their knees, Bobby, Shane and Paul, as well as a few others, on the advice of older siblings swipe more than they can possibly eat. Concealing their hoard on laps beneath the table. Some plates are emptied before grace has been said and, at the furthest end of the table, Martin Murphy is loudly chastised for being a greedy, selfish child. This provokes a teetering mass of crumbling cakes to be returned in haste. The newly ordained Canon Westward from St Jude's Church recites prayers and, following an enthusiastic "Amen", crackers are pulled, tissue-paper hats rustle and rip, and the feasting begins. Paul furtively reloads his napkin with goodies to take home. As time progresses he scoffs three sandwiches, a good portion of crisps and lots and lots of cakes. He also polishes off two bowls of lime jelly. Bloated and slightly nauseous, Paul knows that Christmas has most definitely begun.

At home it is a musty cardboard box that marks the beginning of the festive period. Twelve days before Christmas, the decorations are bought down from the attic in a battered box, a good few years older than Paul. Opening the lid uncovers forgotten wonders. Enthusiastic glee, spread by questions of *remember this,* excite the children. Crêpe paper decorations are unfurled to reveal multi-coloured bells and paper wheels the size of dustbin lids. Creases are flattened. Holes and rips made the previous year by Darren's bow and arrow are crudely repaired using recycled sticky tape, the adhesiveness revived by flames from the fire. Using some rather temperamental drawing pins the five children set to work. It doesn't take much time before the ceilings of the two main rooms become festooned with streamers and balloons. The pins occasionally come loose causing a paper-chain reaction, as crossing streamers drag one another down. In the end it is a mixture of will and determination that holds everything in place. The crêpe canopy appears to lower the ceilings, which brings an extra cosiness to the rooms with the unwelcome void, the coldness of a naked ceiling, cast away. Paul appreciates the additional warmth with a satisfied sigh. So vivid is his recollection of the unpleasant sensation of emptiness that follows when the Christmas decorations are taken down that he allows himself a second, much longer sigh.

Enhancing his joyous mood, the sweet scent of pine permeates. Discovered on scrubland beside the abandoned railway lines near Mark and Jason's school, hacked and dragged along a canal towpath, over fields and through the streets, a real Christmas tree, a festive sight of much delight. Pine needle tracks were left in the snow. When hung with baubles and lights, the bare patches hardly show.

To Paul there is nothing quite like sitting in front of the blazing coal fire, with the tang of Christmas caressing his senses. Reflections flitting over furniture and walls, casting dancing shadows as paper snowmen sway above him. The toasty ambience is further enhanced as painted planks blister and crack in the fireplace, brightening the flames and sending out sparks. The sights, sounds and scents evoking the magic of Christmas touch the entire household. Everyone is jubilantly expectant.

Around this time of year Paul's father reminisces about his own childhood, recounting the sparseness of orphanage Christmases. As toddlers, the orphans would receive a handful of chocolate buttons, as many as they could hold. Which in their tiny tot hands equated to about four or five buttons. He spoke with such joy whenever he retold this particular story. "Even the nuns smiled on Christmas Day," he said, "their cruel tormenting put on hold, in the spirit of all that is good and holy." When older, the children were gifted a book wrapped in newspaper. Unfortunately they never got the chance to read any of these books. They were symbolic gestures to be collected up that very night, never to be seen again — until the following year, that was. Maybe the nuns expected the children to read ten pages every Christmas. Paul asked his father if it made him cry. "Oh no," he replied. "We were just happy to be called out and given a present with our names written on it."

Tales like this make Paul consider how fortunate he is himself not to have been born a century earlier. Mrs Davies has told the class tales of Victorian England, depictions of the unfortunate lives of children. Paul is fully convinced that, as a poor child, he would most definitely have been shoved up chimneys or employed as a mudlark to scavenge in riverbank sediment.

Paul's dad believes Christmas is meant to be a special time for children. Therefore he meticulously plans to ensure that this day of the year is everything it can be. Many months prior he begins buying one or two extra groceries that he stores out of reach in the topmost kitchen cupboard. Paul often climbs on a chair so he can ogle the tinned fruit and canned meats, jars of pickles and bags of nuts. All items set aside for a day so far in the future the remaining time is measured in weeks and not in sleeps.

His dad orders a food hamper from the shopping catalogue, which normally arrives in early December. If the hamper contains chocolates they are taken out to be given as gifts. The children joke that they are for their dad's secret girlfriend, which could quite possibly be true as they never see who gets them. Payment for this lavish Christmas of food, clothes and toys takes between twenty and thirty-six weeks. Instalments that last way longer than the lifespan of any of the toys continue in an unbroken cycle, from year to year.

All presents are wrapped and stowed out of sight. Though not always that well hidden. The packed closet under the stairs may have been a chaotic jumble of worn out shoes and old rags but Paul still locates a gift with Jason's name tag on it. It's heavy and rattles when shaken, an obvious sign that it isn't socks or pants. Lifting a small tear in its corner, taking care not to rip it, reveals no more clues. With his dad in the next room Paul makes sure not to linger, even though he suspects that more gifts might be hidden there. Evoking his father's wrath so near to the day wouldn't be wise.

On Christmas Eve preparations for the following day's feast begin.

"Not one buttt, not one buttt, not one buttt... two." Carole and Paul, whose job it is to peel the spuds, stand side by side at the kitchen sink singing. On Sundays, this song usually makes their chore less of one. "Not two buttt, not two buttt, not two buttt... three." Plop, another skinless tuber is added to the pot. "Not three buttt, not three buttt... not..." On and on they go. Preparing enough roasted and mashed potatoes for seven they need all the vocal encouragement they can muster. Especially as twenty-six fair-sized potatoes is but the start of their mammoth task. Two large nets of Brussel sprouts have them singing way past one hundred. The outer leaves of each sprout are stripped and the base deeply scored with a cross. Submerged in salty water they are left on the stove to be parboiled that evening, along with some chopped carrots.

Sharing the kitchen, and becoming more irate with the plopping of each sprout, Mark punches and huffs. Annoyed regarding the consistency of his dough, he adds more flour, curses and then pours in more water. Hands sticky and gloopy he sprinkles yet more flour into the mixture. Pastry has the power to make Mark fume and even cry with frustration. So it really isn't wise for Carole and Paul to make angry scowls behind his back, but they do it anyway. Persevere Mark does, because he has to, and eventually the home-made mince pies are ready for the oven. Jason's task is to clean the dining room whilst Darren lays the table ready for breakfast.

When the children are tucked up in bed, Dad gets a huge turkey-sized chicken ready for the oven. Blackie's nostrils twitch and Podge obediently sits as Paul's father removes the giblets. Regardless of nutrients and added flavour, these entrails are deemed too unsavoury for gravy and the dogs receive a portion each. Packed with sage and onion stuffing and smeared in fat, the bird is pre-roasted in the oven. During cooking it is occasionally basted in its own juices which ooze out, mixing with the bubbling lard. The waiting sprouts also get a pre-boil.

After a few hours of steaming pans and spitting fat, all is turned off. Precision-timed, ready to be completed the following day, this operation has been perfected over many years to ensure a smooth, stress-free Christmas dinner.

***

Turning over, stretching away the stiffness of a dead sleep, Paul's eyelashes flutter. It had taken hours to nod off, noises from downstairs signifying it really will be Christmas in the morning keeping him alert. Now there's only silence and Darren's shallow breathing. The black, wintry sky is still twinkling, the room dark, yet Paul senses the approaching morning. Despite sunrise being many hours away, it takes but a moment for Paul's inner monkey to voicelessly scream out, "It's Chrrriiissstmaaasss!"

Tied to the footrest of his bed, barely perceivable, hang two bulky socks. Curiosity drags him out from his warm cocoon. A rectangle is cut from the gloom as he hits the light-switch outside his room. Paul attempts to undo the knot that attaches the stocking on his side of the bed. Huffing and puffing, tugging and struggling, he inadvertently wakes Darren.

"It's still night..." Darren moans through barely open eyes. "Go back to bed."

"But it's nearly morning," Paul whispers a persuasive appeal.

"You'll wake Dad," comes Darren's warning, provoked by memories of a previous Christmas. When the children had woken early and gone down to open their presents, it had barely struck four. An annoyed father, whose head had hardly warmed the pillow, yelled down that he would cancel the whole event if they didn't get back to bed. It seemed as though he meant it too, even if it made no sense being as all the presents were there, wrapped and waiting and the food bought and made ready. Adult reasoning continues to confuse Paul. It is hard to fathom spiteful nose-cutting but what is clear is that displeasing their principled father is never a good idea.

At a birthday gathering, one Paul cannot recall, some of the street's children had been invited. As Paul's dad explains it, when it was time to eat, they all rushed and pushed to get to the table. His own well-mannered children stood back, unable to find a seat. This infuriated their father so he evicted the entire party. Apparently, this is the reason the family don't have birthday parties any more.

It is in the hope of keeping his children occupied in their rooms till a more civilised hour that Paul's father has fastened stockings to their bedsteads. It is an ingenious ploy. Paul's determined pulls and yanks keep him extra busy as the knot tightens further.

"Move, I'll do it, give it 'ere." Darren nudges Paul out of the way, and after a couple of huffs and puffs of his own, plus the use of his teeth, he manages to retrieve both stockings. Scurrying like rabbits, the chilled air drives them back beneath the folds of their cosy burrow.

The makeshift stockings contain a handful of monkey-nuts, a tangerine and a chocolate Penguin biscuit. A small hint of the delicious goodies to come. Every year, without fail their father's brother, a distant uncle and only known relative, sends them what they consider to be the real Christmas stocking: a Selection-Box, an assortment of confectionery. Texan chocolate bars, chewy Toffos, Spangles and Smarties, more sweets than they'd eat throughout the year.

The bartering begins. Darren offers up his tangerine in exchange for Paul's Penguin bar. This is swiftly declined without any consideration. Paul is weary of wheeling and dealing with his brothers. His impatient urge to possess certain things has seen his negotiation skills bettered more often than not. So he views every offer, fair or otherwise, with suspicion.

Hearing their chatter, Carole comes in to join them. Mark, in a deep sleep, and Jason dreaming about being pursued by some spear-wielding youths, remain in their beds. Chomping on the chocolate biscuits and monkey nuts, they discuss whether it is safe to venture downstairs.

"Go on, you go first." Darren tries to coax Paul to go down.

"Naw, I ain't... you," Paul parries.

"You said it's morning, not me." Darren jerks his head back and forth while flapping his elbows. "Bwark, bok, bok, bok."

"Suits ya," Paul teases and the two trade blows, good-natured pillow-pounding ones, delivered in the spirit of a very merry Christmas.

"Look! It's morning." Carole points towards the window. The houses beyond begin to illuminate. Ceiling bulbs in upstairs rooms flick on followed by flashing coloured lights at ground-floor level. This convinces all of them it is officially Christmas morning and, therefore, safe to proceed downstairs.

In the living-room, snores penetrate the alcohol-fumed darkness. Bill the lodger occupies the settee. Unable to see clearly, yet too afraid to turn on the overhead light, they sneak inside.

In the low light their pupils enlarge to scope the outline of four clearly separated piles. Their Christmas gifts, all wrapped up waiting to be opened. There is one bundle on each of the two armchairs, another in the far corner of the room and a fourth pile lying on the mat in front of the coal fire. The fifth stack is hidden behind the curtains in the recess of the bay window. Excited whispers soon direct each child to their own pile. Sorting by shakes and squeezes, the soft packages which the children surmise to contain socks and pants are mostly ignored. In the dim light all five senses are utilised. Fingers trace the outlines of strangely-shaped bulges. Ears twitch as shaken contents clatter. Corners are *accidentally* peeled back and prised up, curious eyes squint and peep. Noses sniff and tongues lick to taste the cardboard of the chocolate confectionery boxes. Big packages and the ones that rattle interest Paul the most, for they are generally regarded to have the greatest chance of containing something amazing. It isn't long before Mark and Jason come down to join the three gift guessers.

Their dad also rises. He instructs everyone to let Bill sleep and postpones the gift opening till after breakfast.

Around the pre-laid table they sit, eager to gulp down *their* traditional Christmas breakfast. Cornflakes are only ever eaten on the twenty-fifth of December, and the children associate the crunch and flavour with Christmas morning. Further making an event out of breakfast, there's a special treat of runny boiled eggs and toasted soldiers to dip in them. Unfortunately, the flavour of such delights is not exactly savoured when there's a big pile of whatevers lying in wait to be opened. The fragrant smoke of a Hamlet cigar rises from the head of the table; its welcome plumes curl around Paul's nostrils. Much like essence of pine, cigar smoke is also symbolic of their family's Christmases.

All around excitement, wonder and the odd tinge of disappointment manifest themselves in a cascading flutter of emotions and torn wrapping paper. Paul can't help but to compare. Mark has a Spirograph and a secondhand record player that looks like an old fashioned sideboard. Jason is delighted with his games of Mousetrap and Ker-Plunk. Darren shows off his Buckaroo and a fort with a vast selection of plastic cowboys, Indians and horses. Carole sits upon a Space Hopper whilst opening Katie Copycat, a doll that can write what she does. Paul, not intending to be ungrateful, does consider his brothers' toys to be more exciting than his, although he is delighted with his Action Man. Goaded by a puffy-eyed Bill, Carole laughs and teases Paul for playing with a doll, upsetting their father more than anyone else. Carole gets told off and sent back to bed. It is barely nine-thirty in the morning. She is, however, allowed back down for dinner which is served in the afternoon at around one o'clock. Carole isn't all that hungry for she has devoured her entire Selection Box of ten chocolate bars.

Everyone agrees that powdered soup doesn't taste nearly as nice as tinned. So traditionally cans of Heinz Cream of Tomato Soup are served as a starter. Dished up into bowls, not mugs, and eaten in a more refined manner using proper rounded soup-spoons. After monkey nuts, chocolate, breakfast and more chocolate, any belly rumbles are drowned out well before the first bubble on this day of plenty. Paul's stomach has hardly the capacity for more than one course.

The main meal of chicken follows, and such are the huge portion sizes that everybody, including their dad and Bill, struggles to empty their plates. Despite that, sticking to custom, a stodgy Christmas pudding doused with brandy from the hamper is set ablaze. Dancing blue flames hover over the surface, but its enticing excitement unfortunately is not enough. The pudding cools and remains practically untouched. Paul's dad can't abide waste, so when clearing away the table, it becomes a bone of contention and gets left on the sideboard. Making it nigh on impossible to request more sweet treats later on in the day. Thankfully, this year there is no cabbage water. A mineral-packed salty liquid with gag-inducing floaty-bits, full of iron and therefore far too good to chuck down the sink. Paul dreads it. The stuff makes him vomit so it is best drunk whilst standing over the toilet. Never once has he tilted his mug over the bowl. Be it out of fear or respect, he does not defy his father's command to finish the lot.

Contentment reigns as the Queen's speech comes on the television. Neither a royalist nor a radical, it is tradition that draws Paul's father to the screen. Followed by a cowboy movie, Darren is smitten with his fort and horses. The afternoon is spent playing games on the mat in front of the fire, and nobody is hungry come teatime.

A little while later Paul's dad unscrews the lid on a jar of what looks like caterpillars in slime. It might as well have been the opening of a can of worms for the issue it creates. Who will and won't eat one. Darren chewing proudly announces how delicious they are. Nobody is convinced. Tentatively each child approaches, except Carole who complains about a belly ache.

"Get it down ya neck," commands their father, "it's not going to kill you." Mark and Jason are coerced by the underlying tone of impatience provoked by their dithering. Quickly and painlessly they gobble the fishy maggot. Chewing as though it's sour they swallow and return to the playing.

Paul regrets being so nosey as his dad's focus switches to him.

"Try one!" he says. "Here."

Grimacing Paul backs away.

"I don't like it." His timid whinge does not endear him to his father.

"Don't be such a babby... How'd you know, you ay even tried one."

His father may have a point but Paul can't see it as he has, also, never tried eating dog poo.

"I *really* like 'em, they'm dead nice." Darren's smarmy brag is not voiced for encouragement. "Go on!" Darren urges.

"Just eat it," his dad orders, patience thinning.

He thrusts a cocktail stick beneath Paul's nose. The grey shrimp skewered through the middle wavers before pursed lips.

"Go on, it ay gonna bite ya." Darren sniggers at his own wit.

Paul closes his eyes. Mouth barely open he teases the grubby morsel from the stick with his teeth.

"Pttt, errrr." He spits it out onto the floor.

"Well, if you'm gonna act like a big babby you may as well go to bed now... and you woe be wanting any mince-pies either." More parental logic Paul can't fully comprehend. Still the day is all but over, he's a little sleepy and he's not that fond of mince pies. There is also a sink full of dirty crocks which still need to be washed.

All in all, despite not getting the Etch-A-Sketch he really hoped for, Paul has quite a decent hoard. A blue plastic truck, just the right size for his Action man, and some whirly helicopter discs that zoom around the ceiling by pulling on a cord. There were some indoor skittles and a game of blow football amongst his gifts. A colouring book with felt-tip pens and a black scratchy art thing too. He also got a proper hot-water bottle, as well as the obligatory socks and pants. On the downside there are now three hundred and sixty-five days left till Christmas, and the family will be eating bread and dripping for the next few days.

Chapter Eleven: Spring

By the time spring arrives Christmas, as well as most of the toys, are a broken memory. Carole's Space Hopper was the first casualty. It found a fragment of broken glass out in the street and hissed itself flat. Many key pieces from Jason's Mousetrap game got trodden on or simply disappeared. The glass marbles from his Ker-Plunk rolled away to find holes in the floorboards or were lost in playground encounters when playing marbles *for keeps.* Darren misplaced the saddle from his Buckaroo and eventually, after fiddling around with the spring mechanism, the mule refused to buck. The only gift to survive is Mark's record player stroke sideboard, which is set up in the living room.

Carole and Paul have constructed a makeshift stage behind the curtains in the recess of the bay window. It isn't an impressive stage, one barely big enough for both of them. It's an old kitchen work surface that they found underneath the pigeon pen, raised from the floor using house-bricks. Making sure to slow down the turntable from 45 to 33⅓ rpm, the required speed for long playing albums, they balance *The Best Of Top of the Pops '71* on the central spindle and bring over the secondary arm to hold the disc level. Shifting the play switch they dash behind the curtains to wait for their intro. When the music sounds, they swipe open the drapes. A dramatic rasp from the metal wheels sliding across the curtain-rail introduces them and, with a questionable flourish, they elbow, budge and nudge each other as they sing along to songs like 'Knock Three Times' and one of their favourites, 'Chirpy Chirpy Cheep Cheep'. The irony of vocalising *Where's your momma gone?* as hips wiggle and fingers waggle isn't lost on the motherless children. Carole seems to add relish, imitating the taunts of her tormentors. After bowing to an imaginary standing ovation they normally restart the record and re-dance, re-sing and re-budge one another until reduced to a laughing wreck rolling about the floor. Today the fun is interrupted when Mark pulls out the plug demanding to know who said they could use his stuff. Possessions are somewhat sacred, especially amongst the three eldest, and as sharing hasn't been taught Paul greedily covets most of what they own. He impatiently waits for the day things are handed down. Like tight-knitted woollen jumpers, hand-me-downs rarely stretch to fit his requirements. By the time interest has waned and an item is up for grabs, it has usually lost all functionality.

In the meanwhile, there are other forms of fun waiting for Paul, even from sticks and stones. A majestic tree two gardens away has a low branch for him to sit and bounce upon. He watches the bravest of children parachute through the boughs. From the top branches they lunge themselves off in the direction of another branch a short way beneath. Grasping tightly, the limbs bend and spring, catapulting the children from one branch to another as they steadily descend to the ground. When Paul builds up strength in his arms, he'll be able to hurl rocks from the back garden like his brothers. The glass panes of a distant green-house can be sometimes reached with one almighty lob.

***

Much to Paul's delight, on non-race days like today playing with fire is allowed, providing it is in the back garden and not the house. Inevitably Paul sometimes gets burnt. Not too long ago he was bravely jumping the flames like a Red Indian. Chanting and dancing, circling the fire, paying homage to the returning sun. Similar to a rain dance. His foot got caught in the coiled springs of a smouldering mattress, making him fall just short of the hottest embers. Blackened fingers were slightly scorched and they hurt for hours, but this didn't halt his fascination.

As the spring sun attempts to sizzle the fizzling drizzle, Paul strives too. The wood and damp cardboard collected from about the garden retains too much of its dawn mist and refuses to catch alight. It takes persistence, a lot of matches, sheets of newspaper and some dry rags to encourage the flames to take hold. The sunken seat of a discarded armchair, once his dad's special chair, burns well. Foam melting, blue tongues devour the fabric sending up billows of black smoke. Paul's affinity with fire doesn't spread to smoke. He knows it causes animosity amongst his neighbours. Fortunately, due to the patchy overcast sky and the repeated threat of a spring shower, there are no clothes swaying on nearby washing-lines. Hence a garden fire, even a pungent smokey one, is fine.

A stick is essential kit for every child with a burning desire. Something useful for pushing about the burning pieces, to evoke sparks and to poke at the dying cinders. Armed with half a broom handle, Paul searches for discarded wrappers and plastic bags. Melting them in the fire, he twists them around the burning poker to make a hot molten, flaming torch. Striding across the mountainous terrain, Paul sees himself as a sinister giant. *Vuurt, vuurt, vuurt,* a delightfully wicked sound is created as white-hot drips fall through the air. Decimating the land below, paper fragments and small patches of last year's grass combust into miniature forest fires. Disappointingly the ground is not dry enough for them to properly take hold. A woodlouse scurries away as some worker ants, venturing out into the first rays of spring sunshine, get scalded from above. At first they seem insignificant, their suffering unimaginable until a conscious notion puts a halt to the massacre. Tragic images of sobbing wives and orphaned ants waiting in their ant-homes for a father that doesn't return. Paul's gentler spirit reveals itself. *Vuurt vuurt, k-issh k-issh, vuurt, k-iss*h. Similar to a drumstick tap on a hi-hat. A discarded tin from a steak and kidney pie and traces of last night's rain add percussion to his imaginings. *Ouch!* The stick snatched from him sends a waxy bomb straight to his hand. Unlike blowing on melted candle wax, the plastic tear takes a while to cool. Its sharp, searing pain lingers much longer than his spoilsport brother, Mark, who, grumbling something about it being dangerous, drops the stick into the fire and returns to the house.

Even in the remnants of the fire pit, there are playthings to be found. Charcoal for scrawling, green glass melted treasures to be marvelled at and hidden away and the wiry skeletons of burnt out furniture. The glowing metal spirals deep within the flames pulse between orange to red, hypnotically drawing out daydreams. Obtaining these coiled springs, Paul can insert his toes into the wider gaps and bounce round about like Zebedee off the telly. Though in reality a wobbly hobble is all he can manage. He recalls stumbling more often than not, his foot slipping out, twisting an ankle and sending the spring bounding off, dangerously close to eyes and windows. His growing feet limit the pleasure and practicalities of what had once been a very entertaining pastime.

With imagination in abundant supply, wooden doors, discarded floorboards and a lot of nails can create a palace or, in his brother's case, a criminal hideout. Hovering above a tangle of scrapped bicycle frames, the three eldest have constructed a den near the side gate. Built on stilts when the stinging nettles were dormant, one side rests on the garden wall. A feat of structural engineering that is surprisingly sturdy. Triangular in shape. it fits neatly into the corner, where the back garden of number forty-eight borders theirs. Accessed from beneath by a trap door it has a bolt inside and out. When Carole and Paul are denied entry they can slide the outer bolt across to trap the occupants within. That is if they're *cruisin' for a bruisin'*.

The neighbours at forty-eight are Sikhs. There are not many Indian families in Paul's street, in fact they're quite a curiosity. They speak in a singsong language and fill the air with spicy smells which are alien to Paul. The women wear colourful, draping fabrics with intricate embroidered patterns and, on the heads of the men, turbans. Paul has heard it is sinful for Sikhs to cut their hair. The children cover their topknots with Rumals, white handkerchiefs, for which they are often ridiculed. They are considered to be outsiders.

At the beginning of the spring, when Paul's family were clearing the vegetable patch of rubble, the old grandmother shouted over. It appeared that nobody except Paul could understand what she was saying. She was asking to borrow the rake. Unbeknown to Paul, handing it to her over the fence would result in a tongue-lashing. It transpired that his father, Bill and everyone else were only pretending not to understand and that Paul had ruined their fun. Still, his reward came a short time later when he fell from the roof of the den and landed in the nettles. They allowed Paul into their house and applied a mysterious pink lotion to his stings. The old woman gave him a chapatti pancake to eat which was still warm and tasted sublime. They showed great kindness to Paul, and although not much English was spoken their good intentions soon soothed his injuries.

Now the two families greet each other with smiles. They even sent around a silk outfit for Carole: oyster shell pantaloons with golden threaded swirls around the edges and a matching top. Paul tried to persuade her, said it looked elegant, like a princess, but Carole point blank refused to wear it.

The other local residents are not nearly as tolerant and are quite prejudiced. Paul has never been allowed over any of their thresholds. Regarded as undesirables, many children are not supposed to play with the nuisance family that runs amok, lowering the tone of the street. The battle-lines have been drawn in hopscotch chalk, so to speak. A tenants' association has been formed, headed by the family opposite. Discussions about building renovations and other neighbourly issues are taken up. Top of the agenda: anti-social behaviour. The loudest grievances come from Mrs Chadwick, Paul's other neighbour to the right at number forty-four. Who, it could be fair to say, may have grounds for complaints regarding noise. In a house lacking furnishings the usual stomping and shouting become amplified to penetrate the walls. Perhaps she has her suspicions regarding the mysterious disappearance of her fluffy house-cat. It was discovered hiding under Carole's bed. Perhaps it jumped into the house through an open window, possibly to escape the dogs. It is also quite feasible that Carole carried the cat inside to pet. Regardless, it got shoved inside a potato-sack and driven to some out of the way location to be dumped. Reason being, it scared the pigeons. On race days, a roaming cat would startle the birds and they would flutter back up onto the rooftops. Frustratedly his father would shake his can of dried corn but to no avail, the cat scuppering any chances of winning the much-needed prize money. Miraculously, considering the miles, the wily old moggy soon reappears. It is seen sunbathing on the doorstep, totally unfazed.

Unmindful of parental admonishments, children warned not to mix with those ruffians from forty-six frequently request to join in when a game of *Peep Behind the Curtain* starts up in the cul-de-sac. A basic kindergarten game where one child faces away from a group of slyly, sneaking creepers, all attempting to reach the peeping person's curtain without being seen. The peeper spins around at intervals and anyone caught moving is sent back to the start. Quite limited in entertainment, the game never lasts because the older children sprint rather than tip-toe and fiercely contest any decision to return to the beginning.

Queenie Eye played with a tennis ball is more fun and Paul hears Carole suggest a game of it just as he enters the front garden. There are only five children out in the street today. Kenny and Mandy Cropper from thirty-one, a girl named Pamela and also Debbie, the sister of Martin Murphy, the greedy boy from Paul's school party. Carole is the fifth child and now Paul makes six. Without looking and without spying, Carole gets ready to throw the ball back over her shoulder. Eagerly waiting behind, the rest of them shuffle about. Carole tosses the ball with force and a mad scramble to obtain it ensues. Pamela swoops as it bounces straight past, sweets tumbling from her pocket. An ill-placed Kenny petulantly stamps in frustration as he watches the others dart after it. There's one car parked in the street and the ball slows to a stop under it. With no qualms about soiling his clothes, Paul is quick to drop down and wriggle his way to retrieve the ball. Returning to their position, the ball is obscured and they all sing out, *"Queenie eye, queenie eye who's got the ballie eye?"*

All of the children pretend they're holding it behind their backs. As if the ball, imaginary or otherwise, is a hot potato they fidget with exaggerated awkwardness. Queen Carole, in an attempt to locate the ball, runs at full speed. Ploughing past the children, she hopes to get a glimpse as they are forced to whirl around, continuing to hide what may be behind their backs.

She issues her instructions, "Debbie, spin around." Debbie does a quick twirl, hands zipping from behind her back to her front and back again. Carole sees nothing so moves on. "Kenny, show me your right hand." Kenny feigns some kind of cumbersome battle, as though passing the ball from one hand to the other. He shows his left though nobody notices. Carole makes a decision. "Kenny hasn't got the ball." This annoys him because, regardless of who has it, if Carole had guessed someone incorrectly, that person would have been the next to throw. He strops off to sit on the wall. Paul notices he does this every time he is out or loses a game.

Carole continues in her pursuit. "Pamela, jump up and down two times." She springs and sweets hit the tarmac once more, and this time everyone notices. Carole abruptly calls out "Paul's got the ball," and within the same breath, "can I have one?" Suddenly hands that were hidden are presented beneath Pamela's nose as the children converge en masse. Under duress she gives each of them a lemon sherbet, which almost exhausts her supply. Then she goes home and the rest decide that nobody wants to play *Queenie Eye* anymore. Besides, as Carole has guessed correctly, it will be her turn once more, so Paul isn't too bothered. Instead he concentrates on using his tongue and not his teeth to enjoy his sweet.

Whatever pastime is being played in the street, it is often orchestrated by Carole and Paul, or if it involves older children, one of their siblings. Most kids like to join in a game of hide and seek. Paul always attempts to follow Darren and Jason, who are quite expert when it comes to concealment. They climb over fences, shimmy up drainpipes and hide behind chimney stacks on the roofs. If they don't manage to dissuade Paul in time, he will give the game away by drawing attention to their general location. Probably one of the reasons his brothers rarely join in with the younger children's games More often than not they play much further afield, getting up to all kinds of mischief away from prying eyes. Paul notices his three brothers heading off and, unlike Carole, desperately wants to be involved in their exploits.

He sneaks through Ginger Charley's back garden, clambers over the fence to head them off at the local park. As they round the corner, out he pops.

"Where ya going? Can I come?" Paul's wide-eyed plea receives a standard response from Jason.

"No, get lost!" His glower emphasises that he means business but it falls on ears deafened to such acidity.

"Go on, pleeease let me come?" Paul's baby voice does nothing to endear himself to them. It only bolsters their resolve.

"No, you'm too little, you'll only cry." Jason has neither time nor sympathy for his whingeing younger brother.

"No I won't." A shifty look and sullen pout, as anger and offence knock Paul back. Darren widens his eyes at Mark and Jason.

"Ok, you can come but only if ya can keep up." At which all three bolt away at break-neck speed. Paul is quick to react though slow in pace and soon finds himself, as they predicted, crying.

"Fuckin' bastads!" he screams at their fading silhouettes and slumps to the ground, slapping the tarmacked surface. Grit particles stick to his palms. Dejected he returns via the long way round, back to the street.

***

At this stage of Paul's life there are never enough opportunities to indulge his growing passion for mischief and adventure. School steals away much of his free time, replacing play with constricting rules and organised activities that Paul finds to be a complete bore. Days off never linger long enough to satisfy his breezy soul. No sooner is he free to play out in the street than he is back behind his desk doing writing practice, reading and adding numbers. These lessons, as well as the school terms, drag endlessly on. The periods of respite at Christmas and Easter take an absolute age to arrive and flit by in a flash.

It also seems to rain an awful lot. Through the classroom window the metal climbing frame flickers as droplets of rain glide down the bars. Playtime has been rained-off, replaced by inside voices and no running. Under the vigilant scrutiny of Mrs Davies the last smidgen of fun just got squished. Paul has been ordered to sit, arms folded, at the table with his head down. He was caught switching around the students' coats in the cloakroom, and later crawling about beneath the desks putting to use his lace-tying skills by knotting them to chair legs.

Now, the playground puddles are ringless; scattered sunshine shimmers upon their surfaces. With great excitement, the girls talk about rainbows and rush to the window to peer up at the sky. Paul recalls Carole and himself chasing after one of those arching spectrums. Seeking a pot of gold, they ran up the street, then over the park. The band of colours seemed to dissolve into thin air the closer they got to it.

Once ordered back to their seats the class soon simmers down. Today they are being taught about God in preparation for their First Holy Communion which is due to take place around Easter. The notion of a benevolent, almighty spirit watching over him gives Paul comfort even if God is witness to all of his naughtiness. An extra parent to make up for not having a mom, not a bad trade-off. One feckless mother for an almighty, powerful being. Having two guardians, excluding Bill, is important and makes Paul feel less inadequate, more balanced and on a par with his friends. He does, however, fail to realise that by this reasoning his fellow students also have an extra parent.

Chapter Twelve: Pocket Money

Saturday is generally considered, by many British children, to be Pocket Money Day and on that score Carole and Paul are no different. Their father hasn't the funds so, to obtain theirs, they have to walk that extra mile and there is never any guarantee they will receive some.

With morning chores completed in record time, they practically collide in the hallway in their bid to find one another.

"Shall we go to Mrs McGaveridge's?" Paul voices rhetorically. To which Carole simply sings, "Miss...es Mer Gavridge... Numba, One... Se-ven... One..." Carole has a habit of singing her words and is often chastised for doing so, but in this instance she is purposely singing. Dancing to her tune an overexcited Paul hops from foot to foot like a fool. He is eager to leave before his all-consuming rapture detonates. The thought of sweets and missing out urges him to hurry her along.

Mrs McGaveridge lives next door to St Jude's Church which, although linked with Paul's school, is close to a mile from it. It takes twenty minutes to walk from his home to church, the same time it takes to travel to and from school, which is roughly the same distance between school and church. A triangular circuit of equal distance of which Paul seems to be aware, although he hasn't a watch or a measuring wheel. He has walked these routes numerous times. His class usually strolls down the road to St Jude's Church at Christmas, Lent and on special feast days for mass. Paul has faith and finds comfort in the Lord. The solemn ambience of St Jude's Church fully convinces him that it is indeed, as his teachers say, the holy house of God.

Once upon a time all the family, excluding their dad, attended Sunday mass. Now it is only himself and Carole. The three eldest knock about the nearby graveyard with a mass pamphlet stuffed into their pockets. These date-stamped service notes are shown to their father to imply, or just straight out lie, that they've made an appearance. Paul's brothers have once, or perhaps twice, served as altar boys but as is so often the way, their wickedness surfaced. They would hide up in the balcony and fire pigeon-corn through a pea-shooter, aiming at members of the congregation and plinking them against the gigantic metallic organ pipes. This didn't go down well with the parishioners or the priests and it could have been the reason they were fired.

After receiving the Sacrament of the Holy Eucharist earlier in the year, Bobby and Shane followed the path of their own brothers to join the frocked procession. Unfortunately, and with much regret, Paul's services were not required. The clergymen have long been aware that Paul's family are motherless. Members of the parish often make charitable gestures. Once a year, around Carole's birthday, Mrs Hodges, a cheery old lady on a bicycle, will roll up and knock the front door. For a short period, after Paul's mother abandoned the family and before any of his memories were locked in place, the children were in foster care. Mrs Hodges was Carole's foster mother. She never forgets Carole's special day and always delivers an envelope containing five fifty pence pieces, one for each child. More times than not, as money is tight, it's used for paying bills and buying groceries, though not every time. Mrs Kendal, whose children are pupils at St Jude's, will leave bags of clothes on the doorstep, and around Christmas, men from the church deliver parcels of food and hand over small amounts of cash to Paul's dad.

It's outside the church where Carole and Paul initially met Mrs McGaveridge.

This morning Carole and Paul approach the door with apprehension, afraid one of her teenage sons will answer it and chase them away like beggars. It has never happened, yet the fear is always present. As they creep across her gravel driveway, they huddle together like worried primates. A debate as to who should press the doorbell initiates a Hokey Cokey dance. In, out, in, out, they step about the front door porch. Today it is Carole who is first to shake off her qualms and the inevitable happens. Ding-dong, the doorbell song rings its hollow tune. Waiting patiently for a moment they guess that perhaps she hasn't heard it, so try again, speculating that maybe Mrs McGaveridge is outside in the back garden hanging out her laundry. This convinces them to press a third and then a fourth time. With no response the dejected pair decide to try again later.

Paul suggests that they wait over the nearby Rec, a playground area beside the graveyard. The Rec is limited when it comes to entertaining children. It has no swings, no slide and no see-saw. It does have two concrete playground tunnels. One reeks of urine and the other is strewn with fleshy pages of top-shelf magazines and glass from broken bottles. The jungle-gym climbing frame does manage to occupy the pair for almost ten minutes as they swing about, apelike. Moving on, they look ridiculously awkward ambling about the play area, both hoping their twisted gait of crossed fingers, arms, legs and eyes, though not quite toes, will bring them some good luck. It isn't long before these monkeying antics lead them to a crumbling corner of the playground's surrounding wall. With assistance from a sturdy branch, they hoist themselves up, over and into the graveyard.

Careful not to tread on anybody's grave, they weave around the enormous stone crosses and statues, peering up into the eyes of winged angels, hoping to witness them blink. They read the headstones of beloved wives, fathers, daughters and sons. Discover tiny graves for new-borns and old, moss-covered relics. Some are so ancient it is difficult to decipher the faded markings.

"Arr... look, this one's got no flowers." Carole gazes down to an empty vessel on a neglected grave.

"Yeah... and that one there's got loads." Paul points to a well-maintained plot with potted plants and green glass fragments.

Sympathy strikes them both and they begin a redistribution of what Paul interprets as wealth.

"No, you must only share the plastic ones," Paul informs his sister as she reaches out to a fresh bloom.

"Yeah, cause them ones last longer, doe they?" Carole adds.

"No. It ay stealin' cause them only plastic and we'm just moving um." This makes perfect sense to Paul who guesses that God would also agree that these faded flowers have served their purpose and therefore it is all right to take them.

They continue the mission with a sense of righteous holiness, selecting, thanking and placing the blooms with words of endearment upon lonely resting places. Carole spies a sunken grave, cracked open with a gaping hole, the broken headstone bearing their own family name. Freaked out, they run from the graveyard with muted terror. Only when they are back beyond the broken wall do they release their gasps. Emitting something between a laugh and a scream, they nervously hug one another. Carole suggests that perhaps it belongs to their real dad and at home sits an impostor. Properly spooked, a seed of doubt takes root.

They later meet up with a grocery-laden Mrs McGaveridge as she alights from the bus from town. She allows Paul to assist in carrying her bags and invites the children in for a glass of orange pop and some homemade biscuits. A delightful aroma caresses their nostrils as they cross the threshold. Sweet and buttery; Mrs McGaveridge likes to bake. Before putting away her shopping she rolls up her cardigan sleeves to wash and halve a green apple. Handing them each a piece she then busies about the kitchen. Her naked forearms reveals a crudely scrawled tattoo. Carole has learned of its significance. A jagged line of faded numbers means the kindly Mrs McGaveridge was a prisoner of war. All that Paul knows about the Second World War is that Hitler started it and Paul's dad finished it, when he shot him dead, or so he says. A shadow of doubt hangs over many of his father's tall tales. Such as being a close personal friend of William Shakespeare, whom he regularly misquotes. Historical events as told by his father often conflict with the long-established facts. Paul's dad also insists that he is only nineteen years old.

Before waving farewell, Mrs McGaveridge fishes in her purse for some coins. The children are delighted to receive twenty-six pence each. Rushing off to Bessy's sweetshop, they stop before entering and take a second to consider whether the money is needed at home. It is agreed that, on this occasion, much like the last, it is okay to spend it on sweets. Carole purchases fifty-two half-penny mojo chewy sweets. Paul opts for some white mice, pink shrimps, yellow bananas and stringy red laces. He also buys a gob-stopper and bubble gum.

As the three eldest are not about the house when they return, Paul gets to scoff the lot in peace. Much to his annoyance, a niggling voice urging *just one more* counters any attempt to save some for later. Once all eaten, his greedy eyes seek out Carole. He knows she is extremely proficient at making her sweets last.

Paul is a constant victim to his cravings which easily overpower both will and senses. Want, his insatiable companion, exploits the appetite of Paul's hungry spirit. An invisible imp-like creature that stimulates his taste buds, creating intense yearnings to feed its desires. Hearing the wrappers being torn, smelling the strawberry sugariness, watching Carole nibble, his tongue longs to taste one of her chewy mojo sweets.

"Go on, just one." It is always just one, until the next.

"No, you've had yours." Carole, who has been mothering Paul ever since he cuckooed her naked, wonky-eyed doll from the nest, is a sucker when it comes to his soppy-gazed sulking. Paul knows he can generally coax her when he adds a lengthy plea and a bit more bottom lip.

"Pleeeeeeeease just one... Pretty pleeeeease."

"I'm saving 'em for later." Carole can be strong-willed if she chooses to be. It takes Paul a further eighteen pleases before she relents. Paul, with the tenacity that comes from being the youngest child, could have begged for longer. A lot longer.

They reach an agreement. Egged on by Carole, Paul approaches their father who is sitting doing a crossword puzzle. Grabbing hold of his huge false nose he gives it an almighty tug. To everyone's surprise, it doesn't budge.

Chapter Thirteen: Not Playing Out

School is closed. No more Green Class, no more Mrs Davies, and no more infants playground. The weeks have dragged themselves along and the summer holidays have finally arrived. Next September Paul enters Class Four of the juniors and his break times will be spent in the larger playground with its massive sports fields and steep grass banks. Until then, six seemingly endless weeks of play lay ahead.

It is ten o'clock in the morning and Paul is itching to get outside. Rain has kept him cooped up for all of yesterday and he has grown tired of his sister's company.

"Daad? Can we go to the play scheme over Windsor Park?" Paul's brothers sing their desire in unison. Luckily their father requires a bit of peace and quiet this morning so their regular request receives a standard response.

"Once you've done ya jobs." This produces smiles all round.

The children stand hopeful and wait to be issued with their daily duties. Chores which can range from cleaning the entire house top to bottom including bathroom, landing, stairs and hall, to grocery shopping or even weeding the garden. Mark and Jason get to wash and dry up the crocks in the kitchen, Darren must tidy up the dining room and with Paul's help, Carole is ordered to clean the bathroom, landing, stairs and hallway.

As is typical, the three eldest whip through their tasks and vanish in a flash. Carole and Paul take much longer. Carole starts on the bathroom, which is especially time-consuming due to a grey scum ring that has dried around the bathtub. Vim scouring powder will shift it, but not without vigour and a little added elbow grease which Carole pumps with an imaginary squirt of her biceps. The vacuum cleaner drones loudly as Paul gets cracking on the landing. *Clank, clatter, bang,* the metal aqua-vac goes bounding down the stairs striking the hall window. It doesn't shatter: it can't, as it has already been smashed and boarded up two weeks prior. Paul's dad said it is such a stupid place to position a plate glass window because, unless by some miracle it swerves around the corner, anything dropped on the stairs is sure to bounce right on through the pane. As happened when the dressing-table he and Mark were lugging up to Carole's room released one of its drawers. Disturbed by the racket, Paul's father catches him in the act of dragging the already battered cleaner back up the stairs by the power cord. "No wonder nothing lasts in this bloody house." Paul can guess what's coming next as his dad mounts several stairs at once. Utterance of the word *bloody* shows him the severity of his actions. Only anger and frustration can provoke their father to use foul language. Paul receives a proper smacked bottom and gets sent straight to bed. Resting on top of the covers, aggrieved by his misfortune, Paul has a mini tantrum. Flailing about, heels and fists bounce off the mattress as if being electrocuted. After which he rolls over to inspect the stinging imprint of his father's hand. It shines red, the hot pain dulling to a comfortable warm numbness.

The summer-time sound track of children's laughter, barking dogs, squeals and indistinct voices of those outside aggravates him. He hears Carole yelling "Can I play?" and the front door slamming shut behind her. The house falls silent. Paul pictures his dad downstairs, brooding over his crossword puzzle in the newspaper.

The dancing motion of flies zipping about the vacant light-fitting has a mesmerising effect. Unblinking Paul stares upwards. The sound of the street simmers, way off in the distance a car horn beeps and the shouting of Carole mingles with that of other children as their noises fade away up the road. Paul is regretful that he upset his dad. Sorry for being such an awkward child to a father who is often under pressure. Pressure that could possibly drive his dad up the wall — not only up, but also over it and away. The thought of his dad not being there provokes more tears and remorse. He contemplates life without his dad. Imagines him dying and how terribly lonely he would feel. Paul is now desperately penitent for upsetting his father and, like numerous times before, makes a vow never to displease him again.

Staring at the wood-chip ceiling paper makes Paul feel peckish. It resembles a mass of rice pudding and brings to mind a story called *The Magic Porridge Pot*. The old woman in the book would say, "Cook little pot, cook," and the pot would obey and cook sweet, hot porridge. When she utters, "Stop little pot, stop," the pot would stop.

"*Stop little Paul, stop.*" Life would be a whole lot simpler if, as Mrs Davies said, that type of magic would work on boisterous rascals. Paul reckons he has a lot more nous than the old widow in the story because he would never forget which words to use to halt his naughty behaviour. Although, only when he chose to.

Between the peaks and valleys of sound, Paul can sometimes make out the strokes of the downstairs clock as it chugs like a slow train into the afternoon. His daydreams drift into a doze.

Carole's sing-song voice complaining about having nobody to play with is what stirs him. He immediately calls out, "Daaad?" There is no answer, so he waits for two seconds before trying again. "Daaad... Daddy... Dad?"

His calls are met with silence from his father. He hears Carole filling the kettle and then setting it on the stove. The fingering jingle of the cutlery drawer, the scraping of crockery and chink of a teacup being placed onto a saucer. She is making tea for her father: only *he* drinks from a cup and saucer in their house. Paul tries another round of calls.

"Daddy, Daddy, Dad... Daddy?" Paul could chant for hours; he's had much practice. He is well aware that his shouts must be measured so as not to annoy. If he can get his dad to respond, in the right tone, he is on to a winner.

"Daaad." A further two minutes of moaning calls ensue.

"Daaad... Dad!?." Then jackpot.

"What!" The sternness in his father's voice is to be expected. Paul attempts to soften it with a meek request.

"Can I come dowwwn?"

"No!" Short and sharp though nowhere near the end of his tether. Paul utilises his trump-card.

"But o'm really 'ungry."

Amongst the clatter and bang of kitcheny sounds his father's heartstrings twang. The mention of hunger, providing Paul's wrongdoings are not too severe, is a sure-fire way for him to get released from solitary confinement. His father relents.

"Ok then, you can come down."

Springing into action Paul bolts down the stairs. Forgetting all about his hunger claims, he rushes through the kitchen towards the back door. Carole, who always speaks too loudly, intervenes.

"I fort yow was 'ungry," she bellows.

Paul about-turns, grabs a piece of bread from a loaf on the counter and, halting just long enough to add a squirt of tomato ketchup, pushes the folded piece into his gob. Cheeks bulging, and delivering Carole a resentful nose-scrunch, he continues out the back door.

Over Windsor Park there is no sign of his brothers. Paul hangs about and joins some of the play scheme staff and older children in a game of rounders. After which he looks to the sky, watching the spirals, dips and soars of a kite. Enticing the children to chase about is the kite man, a regular to the park who flies kites that he constructs himself out of bin-bags and green plant sticks from the garden centre. The kite man is extremely friendly. He sends a parachute caught by the wind up the kite-string. Near the top, way above the children's heads, it knocks against a switch. Released, the chute sails down. Twisting and rocking, caught by a breeze it changes direction. The excited children scoot this way and that in a mad race to retrieve it.

Paul soon tires of running about so he decides to hunt for frogs in the brook. The ankle-deep flow of the stream is slow and clean. The rain of yesterday, well on its way to the sea. The bank and water's edge, sucked dry by trees and greenery, allow him to get right down into the gully without slipping over. It is dark beneath the branch canopy. Hidden from the world Paul trundles along, jumping over the central stream as it snakes and bends to follow its natural course. On occasion, where the water swells wide, he has to take a huge leap to switch sides, and in one particular spot a stepping stone is essential for a dry crossing. Today the mossy boulder is moist and Paul's left foot glides on contact. A rumble of pain, brief yet excruciating, shoots through him as he bashes his knee. Cool water fills the gaps between his toes. He pulls up his trouser leg to check for blood but a light pink graze is all he sees. Paul squelches around the brook inspecting known amphibian hangouts. His wet foot allows him to access places normally out of reach. Keeping his dry foot on solid ground, he plunges the wet one into the deep-dish crevices, able now to reach and search beneath the rims of cascading water. A place where Paul lost a frog last spring. The thing slipped from his hands and avoided two further attempts at capture before swimming from sight. Today his search for the escapee is futile. Paul scrambles back up the bank, removes his dripping sock and wrings it out. Hoping to dry it in the breeze, he whirls the sock above his head making rotary blade chopping sounds just like a helicopter. His soggy plimsoll dangles by its lace as he hobbles back towards the street, one-shoed.

Passing by, though not before putting on his damp footwear, Paul calls at the home of Shane, his classmate. He hopes that Shane's father, a formidable church-going character with a voice that booms, isn't at home. Instead his mother answers the door to deliver a milder version of the usual message, "Sorry, he's not playing out!" Next Paul, somewhat optimistically, swings by Martin Murphy's. Sometimes he's to be seen vrooming around the front garden of number thirty-six with his vast collection of Matchbox cars. Today the garden is empty. He briefly considers trying Kenny Cropper from thirty-one. Just like Paul's house, Kenny's garden wall and gateposts form part of the circle that is the bottom of the cul-de-sac. He isn't any fun. Many of the children regard him as a spoilt weakling, a bad loser, who tends to cry far too often. Paul swerves past crybaby Kenny's. Which leaves Charley Blackwell, an aggressive, red-faced, ginger child, who lives opposite in one of the semi-detached houses. Paul has brawled with Charley many times, and although they no longer fight, Paul doesn't particularly like him. Charley's garden gate, at thirty-three, also opens out onto the cul-de-sac. All the houses around the circle have low stone walls with equally-sized goalposts, which, when not obstructed by a football keeper, are used to enter and exit the gardens. Gates is a version of 'one goal and you're out' football, played only in the circle, which is normally devoid of parked cars.

It is unfortunate that, with front windows only metres away from the pavement, shattering shards sound the death knell of many a game. Then the deserted cul-de-sac echoes with angry shouts. Baseless accusations bounce around the circle, aimed in the direction of number forty-six. Tempers flared, the focus of frustrated residents eventually falls upon the abandoned ball. Flung back onto the road after being stabbed by a carving knife, the punctured football hisses and sighs its final breath. In all fairness, other children besides Paul play football in the street and the ball never belongs to him.

Paul decides not to bother calling at Ginger Charley's, instead he chooses to make a stream in his back garden. One half has been dug over for a vegetable patch and planted with potatoes, carrots and cabbages. There are also some radishes and a few lettuces under glass. A small lean-to greenhouse, a mishmash of recycled glass frames, has been assembled against the fence. Through the opaque dimples and frosted panels, tomato plants stoop under the weight of their fruit. Last Easter the children were tasked with clearing away the stones from the newly dug-over ground. They were told to remove all of them, but it was a laborious, impossible task. They extracted masses of builder's rubble and piled it on top of the nettles at the base of the wall. A rocky mound that stretched along the back and side of the house. The seemingly endless chore was only halted due to lack of dumping space. It became a family joke amongst the kids, who, in spite of their grazed fingers, saw the funny side of trying to clear away a demolition site by hand. Covered with soil the piles of rock now form a slope to make a convenient ramp which the children take instead of using the steps. However, this makes no difference to Paul in his endeavours to keep pace with his fleeing brothers.

Paul's dad had also dismantled his old pigeon pen from number twenty-two and, with the help of Darren and Bill, reassembled it in the back garden. Now even bigger it has been extended to house forty birds. Constructed entirely from reclaimed doors and floor-boards, this patchwork shed of various shades is as tall as a double decker bus and equal in length. It has been erected next to the house, right beside Paul's sulking step near the back door and stands directly in front of the chain link fence that separates the adjoining property. It blocks much of the view and casts dark shadows over most of the neighbour's backyard.

A crazy-paved pathway of broken slabs has also been laid. Running parallel with the washing line it slices right through the centre of the plot. Beginning at the foot of Paul's steps, it joins the pigeon loft to the gate at the far end of the garden. A grey stone border that separates the orderly rows of vegetables from the unkempt brambly chaos opposite. In amongst the overgrown grass, a dangerous tangle of buckled bicycle wheels and abandoned shopping trolleys lie in wait for clumsy stumblers such as Paul. Scorched mattress springs blackened by flames occupy the centre of a large charcoal circle.

Paul uses a spade to cut away a strip of turf. It is hard going chopping through the well-established clumps. Worms keep getting in his way. Although it is common knowledge that halved worms live on as two, he removes many by hand because cutting through them seems too cruel. This hinders his progress. He isn't so conscientious, the unfortunate earthworms that he overlooks get sliced by the blade. Squirming and recoiling, apologies are uttered yet the massacre continues as he digs out a trench in line with the path on the unkempt side.

Creating a four-metre groove which is half a metre wide and just as deep occupies much of his day. He lays the hosepipe from the tap of the kitchen sink, through the open window, over the wall and down the slope. Bursting into life it jerks and bulges, unfolding with the flow of water and, like an angry serpent, it splutters and spits before spewing out a steady stream. Given time the channel begins to fill up but as soon as he turns the tap off, the water disappears. Paul can't figure it out. It takes a while for him to consider that maybe the gully will never become a proper stream and gallon upon gallon is wasted in his attempt.

From the back garden Paul hears a disturbance out in the street. People are yelling and Blackie is barking. Podge has a cat in his jaws and is frantically shaking the life out of it. The sight is distressing, the sound horrendous. No amount of screams or swipes will make Podge release the squalling kitty. Paul's father comes out, throws a bucket of water at them and the cat dashes to safety beneath a nearby car, dismissing the remonstrations of irate onlookers with a dispassionate comment about the nature of dogs. For him there is no question about allowing Blackie and Podge to run free: it is a fact that in working-class areas dogs do roam. After a strong word to Paul about leaving the hosepipe running, he returns to his game of chess. Paul is shaken up by the harrowing scene. Witnessing the powerlessness of the cat and the savagery of his own pet. The sounds and images leave a deep imprint.

Soon after, one Sunday afternoon, Paul's dad, with Bill walking three steps behind, comes home from the Beckley Tavern. He is holding a tattered rope and leads a vicious Alsatian into the house. Snapping and cowering, it growls and yaps. The dog has been terribly mistreated. Slinking low to the ground, its backside appears sunken and its hind legs have hardly the strength to walk. With flashes of fear and ferocity it appears to be frightened by everyone and everything, except for Paul's dad. It's possible to count its ribs through the balding fur and calloused skin. It's so starved it can't stomach solid food so Paul's father feeds it up ever so gradually with bowls of Weetabix mixed with water. The downstairs lavatory is given up to house Red, a name chosen to match the colouring of his coat.

It takes weeks to win Red's trust, which is not given freely. In the kitchen, when Red is introduced to Podge they fight, and although they are immediately separated without injury, Podge relinquishes his position and saunters away. Paul doesn't see him again. Blind Blackie also wanders off. He makes the local newspaper with the headline 'Home Plea for Blind Blackie'. When Paul's dad goes to fetch him, he is informed about some enquiries from a loving family. One with plenty of space and money to pay for a cataract operation. Blackie sees out his last days away from the concrete and glass of the backstreets, retiring in comfort on a farm. Or at least that's the official line told to Paul.

Chapter Fourteen: Made-Up Games

Grey rainy days often disrupt Paul's summer-time play. Gazing through the trickles on the windowpane, his exasperated breath momentarily clouds his view. Tracing his emotions, his finger adds a frown to the glistening face depicted in front of him. With a swipe it is gone to reveal an empty street and, to his dismay, lively puddles. He begins to sing. "Rain, rain, go away, come back another day." Repeating it, over and over, and then over again. Perhaps this is the 'another day' as he has sung this rhyme many times before.

He decides to quit, to occupy himself with making a den beneath the dining-room table. He gathers up the seat cushions from the sofa, leans them against the legs of the table, holding them in place using dining chairs turned on their sides. What he really needs to make a super dark den are heavy curtains, something the family have in abundance.

In his search of these materials Paul rummages in the hallway closet, a small cubbyhole set within the recess underneath the stairs. By order of his father, everything "that may come in useful" gets dumped in there. A load of old clothes, stuff the rag and bone man, if he ever came around, would happily exchange for a balloon or perhaps a goldfish. Usually one on its final fin, a side swimmer, that rarely lasts a week. Mostly it stores away junk, seldom-used tools, broken furniture, worn out shoes and of course rags, piles of them. An unscalable cloth mountain that reaches up to the highest point of the sloped ceiling. Releasing the latch on the cupboard door creates a fabric avalanche. Accompanied by dust and the aroma of Kiwi boot polish, the cascading mound swallows up Paul's feet. In a vain attempt to contain the deluge Paul pushes, shoves and leans into the pile, his changed mind set on closing the door. A familiar woollen jumper settles upon his head. With contempt he tosses it aside, recollecting how itchy it is. Last time he wore it he couldn't get it back over his head. He had to ask his dad for help and the blasted thing nearly tore his ears off.

The tumbling heap continues to collapse out of the door. Paul fights with determination, squashing, pressing, kicking and, at the same time, manoeuvring himself backwards into the hall. The battle against gravity is lost though he doesn't yet know it. Shoulder to the door, hoping sheer force will squeeze it shut, his stockinged feet slide on the plastic flooring. He fights against it for a while but, with no other option, yields. Stepping aside the door swings fully open and out gushes half the contents of the closet. An instant later, on his way out the door, Paul's dad crosses the hall.

"Good to see someone using their initiative, can't find a thing in there."

Understanding the assumption, Paul does nothing to correct his father's praises. Instead of building his den he spends two hours rearranging the clutter whilst his siblings venture outdoors beneath a clearing sky.

Paul comes across a metal lid from a biscuit tin, recognising the floral pattern from that of a container he'd seen a thousand times. In the blink of his eye, a flickering spark flashes a bright idea. He immediately heads to the sideboard in the living-room to retrieve the receptacle from amongst the odds and sods. Placed inside are important documents such as medical cards and christening and birth certificates. Delving deeper beneath tattered Green Shield stamps and old cigarette coupons, he pauses. His imagination drifts over colourful images of motorcars and aeroplanes depicted on Brooke Bond tea collecting cards. A selection of dog-eared photographs lay in the bottom. Creased black and white memories of his dad's time in the army. As he empties the contents into a second tin, which is also without a lid, Paul spies a wedding photograph. A faded, long shot with washed-out faces, his father and mother on the steps of a building. He can just make out his mother's teeth which are goofy like Carole's. He discards the image to continue with his new plan. Paul has decided to create a treasure chest for all his prized possessions.

In no particular order he includes the following: a selection of cat's-eyes, ball-bearings and king-sized marbles. A magnifying glass and an incredibly sharp single-bladed penknife that is excellent for shaving sticks. A slightly bent six-inch nail. Also a tiny flashlight bulb and a nine-volt battery: a quick lick tells him it still works. From under his bed he obtains a string of rosary beads and his First Holy Communion medal, which Paul considers sacred as well as precious. Next comes a plastic troll with pink hair, a keyring he found in the park and a pipe-cleaner man he made at school. Adding a magnet tied to a piece of string causes him bother. He struggles to lay the items neatly. The metal tin, bearings, battery, bulb, nail, knife and pipe-cleaner man gather in a clump unable to resist its pull. He rolls the magnet up in rag to make it dull but the attraction is still too strong.

Almost satisfied, Paul seeks out one final item, something special to add value to his trove. Not exactly stealing, more borrowing without consent, he selects a rather small, insignificant pepper-pot from out of the sideboard. A ceramic, painted pot depicting a Geisha that he'd heard his dad say might be worth something one day. Again the memory of Carole falling off the dining table and bashing her lip comes forth because this was amongst the items they were squabbling over the day the donkey head rolled off the table, with Carole following behind. Being a most impressive addition to his collection, he conceals it within an old sock for protection. Content with all his valuables, he sets about finding a suitable hiding place in amongst the tidy mess of the cubbyhole.

Lightbulbs are only inserted where essential in rooms such as the living room or kitchen, or in strategic areas such as the upstairs landing, where one bulb can illuminate three bedrooms. A cubbyhole dumping ground does not merit such a luxury. Therefore when Paul closes the closet door behind him he fumbles around blindly, swallowed by darkness. It takes a while for his squint to adjust to the fine vein of daylight underscoring the door's position. Parting the fabric stacks with one hand, he struggles to squash his cache into the weighty tower of cloth whatnots. Eventually, opting to insert it closer to the summit, he obscures the biscuit tin within a sweater. Once a favourite item, he laments the day mangy Mary Boswell gobbed on his best top. Yellow stringy spit that he thought toxic. He ran into the house crying, took the sweater off and never wore it again.

Once Paul has stashed his treasure trove, he draws a map marked with an X and sets about writing clues for its location. Several pieces of paper are scrawled on with instructions such as to look under Dad's cushion, where he places further written directions to look within the rip of the carpet on the bottom stair. There awaits another scrap to send the treasure seeker running up two flights of stairs to search behind the attic door. The more notes he writes, the better the hunt will be. These clues are solely for Carole. Paul doesn't trust the three eldest not to claim some of his treasures for their own. They also have a tendency to discover his hidden messages out of sequence, skipping the correct order, which isn't part of the game.

Carole, a willing participant, plays along nicely and Paul follows her from attic to kitchen to dog's toilet to outside to all about the house with a satisfied gleam in his eye. When she finally enters the cubbyhole a cunning Paul ha-ha's like a pirate and shuts her inside. Carole bangs on the door, screaming something about the dark. When he releases the latch the force of her escape crushes him between the door and the wall. He's trapped, and Carole metes out sufficient jabs and tickles to punish his treachery.

***

The dark can be quite frightening to young children. Fear has the power to silence gasps and steal away your breath. Playing *murder in the dark,* a creepy game, both thrills and terrifies Paul. Typically played on a rainy day, when their dad is out of the house, the children, using heavy blankets and curtains, block every window to make the house pitch-black. They sort out some playing cards, one for each participant, descending numerically. An ace to represent the murderer and a king for the detective. Should the king meet an untimely death, the holder of the queen will then become the detective, unless of course she too is murdered. Then it will fall to the holder of the next highest card. A hushed, eerie vibe descends upon the scene as the children huddle beneath the naked lightbulb to draw lots. Careful not to show anyone, discreet peeps inform them of their role. Once ready, the light is turned off and the players slip away to creep and sneak about the gloom. There are not many rules: no hiding together, victims must lie down on the ground and not give the game away by telling. Also, try not to laugh.

The choice role is that of the murderer who slinks about without fear to locate victims. Sometimes deftly silent and other times quite vocally expressing ghostly woo's and monstrous grr's for good effect. Carole, prone to giggling herself to death, bites hard on her knuckles. Once found, a good measure of strangulation or a simple tap on the shoulder uttering the words "You're dead" will make the victim lie down, stiff like a corpse. If anyone stumbles across a corpse they nervously enquire "Are you dead?" hoping that that person doesn't respond with "No… but you are." Relived to be finding a victim and not the real murderer lying in wait, the discoverer then yells out "Murder in the dark!" and the lights are switched on. The survivors gather downstairs where the detective begins an investigation. Asking questions like, where were you, what did you hear, and who do you think the murderer might be? Only when the detective states clearly who they think the murderer is does the truth *have* to be told. It is a simple game, one they all enjoy playing, but it rarely goes further than two rounds before accusations of dishonesty spoil the fun.

Rules are often tweaked or broken. This bunch of mavericks make most of them up as they go along. Inventing sports like Socky, an unsophisticated game using extra whiffy socks. Human targets with arms stretched wide open stand some distance apart. Taking turns they lob pongy socks back and forth across the arena. Wafting these anti-air-fresheners about the bedroom creates a proper stink, one able to produce convulsions and draw tears, although it isn't always entirely clear whether they are fits of laughter or just fits. Wherever the sock-bomb strikes, it must be held there and endured for a full count of ten seconds. So it is advisable to contain hysterics and to keep your gob firmly shut, unless partial to picking dog hairs off your tongue. Bravely or stupidly, Paul tempts Darren with many free shots at his gaping mouth. Darren, thunderbolt fast and a crack-shot, hits the target on numerous occasions leaving Paul spitting feathers and various dusty particles.

For those with a creative mind, making up activities to pass the time comes as second nature, more so after the death of toys. A game of kicky-swing over the back park is a much more savoury way to tick away tedium than a smelly round of Socky. Although for full enjoyment kicky-swing does require a minimum of three participants. Paul recalls playing it with only Carole, a boring experience that had him chasing his own tail like a crazed duffle-coated retriever. To play all that is needed is a playground swing and a football. Even a burst-leather casey will suffice. The fun part, as far as Paul is concerned, is owning the swing. All other positions, except bowling, induce grumbles and extreme bouts of yawning. The kicker, sitting on the swing as standing is not allowed, often thrusting their legs forwards and drawing them back in a manic bid to gain as much momentum in the quickest time possible, prepares to strike. Hopefully they are ready when the bowler tosses the ball. Simple rules: kick the ball as far as possible, and if it is caught, you're back on the floor. The more catchers scattered about, the more difficult it is to stay in the chair. As is the way with most street games, forceful kids often cheat. Squabbles erupt. Claims from the kicker that they hadn't actually touched the ball. That it had struck the chain or the base of the swing prior to being caught. The smallest children always have to wait an eternity for a turn and most of them are immediately caught out because they don't manage to swing high enough before striking the ball. Tears and tantrums follow, but not from Paul. He is a fast wiggler who knows to hit the ball straight down until he has the power to send it flying through the air.

***

The back park, constructed on a triangular piece of wasteland, lies beyond Paul's road. Ginger Charley and neighbours like Kenny, who live on the opposite side of the street, can simply jump their back fences to gain access. Paul, when he doesn't sneak underneath Charley's kitchen window to vault over the bordering wooden enclosure, has to go all the way around or take the passageway at the bottom of his garden. Thanks to Bill's training he can sprint up the alley, through the estate of maisonettes that skirt one side of the park and be there in under four minutes. Even so, when shadowing his siblings a few minutes is more than enough time for them to vanish. So coming face to face with Charlie's growling dog is a risk he often takes.

Making up the third and furthest edge of the park's triangle plot, separated by a knee-high meadow of uncultivated grass, tower the barb-wire perimeters of private houses. Where, beyond the grasp of scrumping hands, apples bob temptingly on wind-brushed branches. In the centre of the park, sunk within a grassy hillock, lies a massive crazy-paved hollow, or as Paul sees it, a huge mosaic bowl left behind by a forgetful ogre. This slab-encrusted play area has a steel slide that starts at the top of the rim and slides right down into the bottom of the basin. It reflects the sun, dazzling like an enchanted sword which, in the heat of summer, is often much too hot to touch.

Slide cricket, a variation on his father's favourite sport, is also enjoyable. It's mostly played by the bigger kids as it is much more strenuous than kicky-swing. It has clear rules and so generally produces fewer arguments. Similar to normal cricket there are fielders, a wicket-keeper, a bowler and a single batsman, of sorts. From the foot of the slide, the ball is bowled up to a player standing at the top. It is kicked with the intention of sending it as far as possible, preferably clear out of the concrete bowl that is the main field of play. Doing so awards the batsman, or woman, six points and, just like in cricket, if it touches the floor before crossing the boundary, you only get four points. Single runs are obtained by sliding to the bottom. Dashing back up to the top rewards you with a second point. If the ball is caught or strikes either end of the slide before the player reaches the *crease* to proclaim themselves *in*, they are out. After a few *overs* of scrambling up the steep bank, children declared out are normally too knackered to complain.

Also contained within the base of this giant's dish, in addition to the swings, stands a metal climbing frame which is ideal for playing tick-off-ground, a variation of tag where the participants are not permitted to touch the floor. There are also a couple of free-standing brick walls. Erected at opposite ends, white, dribbling, gloss-paint marks-out the outlines of two goal-posts. Scrawled graffiti depicts the initials of the town's football club, stating how they rule, *Elvis Is King* and, in bright yellow, a misspelt racial slur intended to offend.

***

By now the rain has almost completely dried up. With neither a soul in the street nor a peep from the park, Carole and Paul decide to amuse themselves with a game *they've* created called Frisbee Castle. This they play on the front garden using any plate-shaped item they are able to skim through the air, preferably one that hovers like a flying-saucer. Starting from the doorstep they call out "Green Land," meaning the patch of grass in front of the house. Paul aims to skim the disc, a lid from a can of emulsion paint, onto any part of the grass, ideally close to Tin Land. Running to retrieve it, he stands on the very spot and then shouts out "Tin Land." Either of the two manhole covers in their garden constitutes the province of Tin Land. A light, skillful toss is normally enough to touch down on target because even resting on the outer edge of the manhole cover qualifies. "Slabs," Paul calls out as the next location. The pathway leading to and around the house becomes a lonesome dusty trail, known as Slabs. Paul is prudent to aim his throw in line with the path. One awkward bounce can send him off the beaten track to forfeit his turn to an ever-eager Carole. The long distance to the front gate merits a second shot on Slabs before the annoyingly tricky Castle Gateway. For this shot to count, the lid must rest on the step between the gateposts. Castle Wall is the final triumph, requiring an easy, cheaty, lean-over dropping action that is hardly a throw at all. If the disc remains balanced on the battlemented wall, anywhere past the third upright block, the castle has been conquered and the game is complete. Rule variations and other locations are added from time to time, meaning the children occasionally invade neighbouring lands to conquer more castles in nearby gardens.

It is almost teatime and children's telly is about to begin. Paul's dad has returned and is inside staring intently at the black and white set. He is watching the snooker and needs to concentrate, to follow the movement of the balls as most of them appear grey. As the children enter the room the coin-operated television switches off. It has run out of credit which means no cartoons.

Chapter Fifteen: Conflict

Though it never fully went away, the rain has returned. Paul feels it is terribly unfair since this is technically the summer holidays. Six weeks of fun and freedom has, for the most part, been a washout. Rain is never any fun. Working-class children like Paul don't splash in puddles, not unless they're looking for a thick ear.

Tasked with tidying the living-room, Paul uses a damp cloth to wipe away a dusty outline left on the sideboard. The television has been returned to the shop, partly because Carole and Paul whinged too loudly about missing *Pipkins*, one of their favourite television shows. Also to blame were the entire English cricket team for drawing against Pakistan, again. Watching the cricket often annoyed their father, putting him in a bad mood. As money was tight, he decided it just wasn't worth the rental fee, claiming there was never anything decent to watch on the damn thing anyway. So back it went. It had a coin-operated meter attached to the back to pay for the leasing. An employee from the electrical shop on the main road would call around to empty it. However, the lock had been picked by one of the three eldest, though not without the knowledge of their father, so there was never enough money inside it to cover the fee.

Times are particularly hard at present and it seems that purse-strings are being knotted in many homes, not just Paul's. It's commonplace to borrow money until the family allowance can be collected from the Post Office, often relying on favours from pub mates or pigeon-fancier colleagues just to tide them over. Alas, everyone Darren is sent to ask claims to be brassic.

So when a bullet-sized hole inexplicably appears in the dining room window, a sheet of glass larger than Paul, there just aren't the funds to replace it. Covering it up with a big piece of board like the back door will cast gloom about the room. Therefore the silvery cracks spreading from the hole up towards the topmost corners of the pane, are held together using long strips of sticky-tape. Airtight it is not as the adhesive tape only clings sporadically and quivers annoyingly. Whenever the wind howls outside, the window responds with a whistle and when the front door closes the shaking glass clatters, threatening to shatter. The thought of this happening worries Paul.

This make do and mend mentality of his father's generation cares little for cosmetics, as is evident all about the house. When the mismatched stair carpets, of which there are three different off-cuts, wear-out and rip, they are simply nailed down to prevent tripping hazards. A broken light-switch, still functioning perfectly well, is left open. Paul, reaching out in the darkness, his fingers slipping behind, finds a live connection. A numbness shoots through his whole frame, and he feels like he's been struck by God. The sudden shock makes him blurt but does no harm. Newspaper does exactly the same job as puppy-soft toilet rolls. So what if the ink smudges when you wipe. "We can't afford to flush away money." Minty toothpaste with the lovely coloured stripes? Salt cleans teeth in much the same way. Chipped teacups, cracked plates and bent forks will still deliver nourishment to a hungry belly. In Paul's house nothing is wasted and things are rarely thrown away. The cupboard under the stairs, the one near the back door, the sideboard and various junk drawers overflow with *might-be-usefuls*. Paul notices how quickly the clutter gathers, the chaos of which also bothers him but only when he pauses to recall what he saw before. A clean, spacious cupboard, with a closable door. It doesn't seem to annoy anyone else, and he forgets about it when he is playing out.

Many of the street's occupants consider Paul's family somewhat unsavoury. Mrs Chadwick, from number forty-four, is very vocal in her dislike of the ruffians that reside next-door and they often come up as a subject of discussion in meetings of the tenants' association. Adding paper to the flames, Red has bitten her grown-up daughter, who happens to be a policewoman. There is a heated debate; talk about having the vicious mutt put down. Killed for a nip that drew hardly any blood by a dog who was technically on its own property. Both semi-detached houses share a common gate and a length of pathway that splits left and right, like a two-pronged fork just in front of the houses. Red bolted through the door, which had been left ajar. The chomp took place on the shared slabs, on the dusty trail close to Castle Gateway. Luckily this was Red's first offence so a warning was issued that next time he would have to be destroyed. To Paul it was an incomprehensible notion to punish a guard dog just for doing, albeit mistakenly, what it was bred to do.

Paul and Red share a special bond. Paul has spent many sulky moments sitting on the top step out back in the company of Red's sympathetic nudges and licks. Red is non-judgemental and an excellent listener. When he first arrived all emaciated, matted and abused, he growled at Paul's elder brothers. Yet never at Paul. His dad often marvelled about the way Red would search the house from top to bottom trying to locate Paul. Sniffing him out from under a bed or tracking him to the closed closet door. Noisy nostrils snuffling beneath the gaps of the door would make Paul's suppressed laugher burst out, confirming what the dog already knew.

It is a harsh existence for Red. He spends all his days attached to a chain in the back garden and his nights shut behind the door of the downstairs toilet. He is rarely taken for walks but, on the odd occasion, late at night after he's been to the pub, Paul's dad will take Red for a stroll around the football fields. With no people to bite or dogs to fight it is quite safe to allow him off the chain for a run. Paul is also somewhat negligent. When life is going well he happily skips past the dog on his taut chain, ignoring Red's wagging requests for a stroke. The loyal hound holds no grudges, and when Paul requires comfort he is always there ready and waiting, panting happily.

Close allies to Mrs Chadwick are the Wright family from number thirty-five. The mother, a robust, opinionated woman with seven children, all too old to play with Paul, chairs the meetings of the tenants' association. Paul's dad hasn't attended any of the gatherings. He's never been invited. He says the Wrights deem themselves a cut above the rest because they own a car. Not many people do on Paul's road. They've knocked down their garden wall and crazy-paved over a good portion of the grass so the car doesn't have to stand out in the street. The football is forever finding its way into their garden now, and if the children don't quickly sneak in to retrieve it it's slashed with a knife. On occasion the boys from both families have clashed; verbal assaults exchanged and noses bloodied. It is fair to say with smashed windows, burst balls and black eyes there is not much compromise with regard to letting the living live. The police have been called at times. The Wrights have a telephone which, along with owning a car, is regarded as a bit of a status symbol amongst many of the working-class residents. Paul is well aware of which households have a car or own a telephone. He knows which families go on summer holidays and those who receive chocolate eggs at Easter. Whenever the chimes of the ice-cream van sound, he knows which kids will dash into their houses and rush back out to buy ice-creams, before the van moves on up the road. The Wrights, they seem to have it all.

***

Not long after the hole in the window appears, a couple of the Wright brothers and a selection of skin-headed youths gather in the street for a showdown with Paul's family. Bill spots them outside Kenny Cropper's house, glaring over. It is clear they are trying to psych themselves up to knock the door. On the other side of which, Paul's dad waits and just as they raise the flap of the letterbox to knock, he swings open the door. Red charges out barking, snarling and snapping at the air. The panicked callers scatter like a spilt tin of marbles. Not knowing which bottom to bite, Red is quickly called back inside before he has a chance to sink his teeth into any of them. The gang, who haven't quite given up, regroup outside number thirty-one. Their father tells Carole and Paul to stay indoors and they watch out of the window. The rest of the family stand united on the front garden, their nerves well hidden behind scowls and glares. Bill, as cool as a polo-mint, walks straight over, grabs from one of them a large wooden club, and, pounding it in his open palm, offers to take them all on. They decline and then disperse.

Afterwards Paul takes to hiding a claw-hammer behind the gate at the bottom of the garden, fearful that he may get ambushed as he walks the back alleyway. Paul often feels scared and runs past certain houses to avoid conflict. He is terrified of the deaf girl up the road, ever since she got in his face in a fit of anger and shouted incoherently before walloping him across the head. Out of fear he also avoids the boy with the yellow-gunky lifeless eye, the girl with chapped, cracking skin and the black kid who skips alongside passing cars, punching his knee as though papping a car-horn, shouting "Beep-beep beep-beep" and repeatedly calling the drivers "Camel".

Paul has no understanding of those he so often hears referred to as spastics and mongols. His unchecked ignorance is in danger of manifesting into a form of prejudice. At a summer fair, whilst hacking through a jungle of adult-sized limbs to get near the stage, Paul bumps into a midget. The sheer terror he feels, peering into the startled eyes of a large-headed dwarf who aggressively shoves him out of the way, shakes Paul to the core and makes him bawl. Even people who limp or have a slight hunch cause him alarm. Paul simply doesn't trust that they won't suddenly veer towards him and attack like a raved lunatic.

Conflict is a prominent feature in Paul's everyday existence, be it physical or mental. At home he clashes with Carole and his older brothers over possessions. In the school playground he battles for inclusion. Out in the street or over the park many squabbles end with a bop to the nose. Even sleeping he struggles with bladder control and is frequently plagued with nightmares. Adding to this he fights a private war to suppress memories, hiding a misguided sense of shame attached to events that he pretends never happened. Coping with his hard-knock life, Paul is unconsciously constructing a toughened exterior. A mischievous expression, a smile to belie his anguish.

After cleaning the front room, Carole and Paul are ordered to tidy the clothes heaped behind the wardrobe doors in their bedrooms. Considering that the children mainly wear their school uniforms, there is an awful lot of clothes that need folding. Trousers that don't fit, bundled together with masses of t-shirts and pullovers that reveal belly buttons. Working as a team to halve the task, they pull all the items out onto Carole's bedroom floor in order to sort them. They make a game of it. Dragging everything out of overstuffed drawers they toss the clothing up in the air like autumn leaves and bury themselves in the mounds.

Paul becomes one with the heap. "Can you still see me?" his muffled voice enquires. "Can ya?"

Carole remains silent. Popping his head around the door to view a room covered in fabric, Paul's dad responds. "Yes, I can see you, now stop messing about and get on with it." His exasperated tone lacking its usual punch is still enough to put a halt to their shenanigans. However, two hours later the house is completely silent. The clothes remain a tangled jumble.

Chapter Sixteen: Another Home

Unquestioning of his altered predicament, Paul stands alongside Darren and Jason in a large lounge-playroom. He isn't concerned with the absence of his eldest brother, Mark, but wonders as to the whereabouts of his sister. A middle-aged man with friendly brown eyes and bushy brows introduces himself as Malcolm, the head supervisor. Paul hears nothing of the conversation that follows. Instead his gaze wanders around a space that is clean and orderly. Squeezed into a corner, next to a door marked 'Fire Exit', is a small classroom. Bright toys and toddler-sized furniture indicate it must be a kindergarten. A red-carpeted area, partitioned off by low shelves stuffed with books, provokes in Paul a nostalgic memory of Yellow Class story-times.

Children playing outside jostle to get a view of the newbies through the glass panes in the fire door. Small, medium and large, like *matryoshka* dolls, the three brothers stand side by side, arms outstretched holding a bundle of clothes. A dark-haired child in his early teens knocks at the window. "Oi, that's *my* jumper!" His annoyed heckle stirs up much laugher amongst the gawping pack gathered around him. Paul doesn't have a clue what is going on: from messing about tidying clothes in Carole's room to here, wherever here is, in a couple of hours. No one has given him an explanation, or if they did, it was done in such a way, perhaps to lessen the impact, that he hadn't grasped that he is now in what his dad has so often referred to as "the cottage homes": an orphanage called Waybrook House.

Despite the uncertainty, Paul is glad that he didn't have to finish the chore of folding all those garments. Instead he is waiting in line to receive a fragrant pile of freshly laundered clothing. He is given a pair of brown corduroy trousers, which appear large enough to easily cover his ankles. To hold them up, a red and blue snake-belt with an S-shaped clasp. Children Paul's age regard snake-belts as super snazzy. Crybaby Kenny from number thirty-one has one, as does Martin Murphy from number thirty-six. Paul can't wait to show off his. He also receives a dark green V-neck pullover and a pale green shirt, with rounded collar-tips, some clean underwear, a vest, numerous pairs of socks which are free of holes and a brand new pair of plimsolls. Next Malcolm hands him a checked burgundy dressing gown made from a coarse heavy fabric, some diamond-trellis pyjamas which are orange, a face-cloth and a blue plastic cup with a matching blue toothbrush.

Malcolm leads Darren and Jason away to be housed with the older children. Paul is left alone in the charge of a second, lightly greying, younger man. A uniformed police officer. Paul quite likes coppers, although when playing cops and robbers he always opts to be a robber as being chased is much more fun. He's met many. At school, PC Spoon came to give talks, and at home to follow up on complaints and issue warnings. When toddler Paul wandered off, he was driven home in a police car, and when his father attended court, for some misdemeanour, he offloaded his tribe of five, very active kids in the police station. Unbeknownst to the officers, he gave the children permission to play up as much as they liked. The children spent a good portion of the morning getting under the feet of flatfoots. Paul recalls being chased around by a jolly sergeant and clambering over desks. The officer's attempts to calm the kids down with a bribe of sugary sweets failed. Meanwhile Paul's father was pleading his case. Angry at his perceived injustice, he instructed the judge to take his kids into care saying he already struggled to feed them, so there was no way he could afford to pay a fine. Subsequently, he got off lightly and was able to relieve the officers of their babysitting duties.

The policeman escorts Paul to a communal bathroom. A large echoey space with a high ceiling, no windows and masses of water pipes that run across the walls like train tracks. A wooden shelf with slotted compartments spans the entire length of one wall. Paul is allocated an empty slot in which to deposit his blue toothbrush and cup. He delights at seeing a row of multi-coloured cups with matching brushes. In Paul's house there isn't a great deal of tooth brushing going on.

He'd once been the proud owner of a Donald Duck toothbrush, a brand new one given to him by his dentist. For Paul's initial visit to the dental clinic, the dentist instructed him to bring along his toothbrush so he could be taught proper tooth cleaning techniques. He took the brush he most preferred, a red see-through one. He enjoyed squinting through its plastic shaft; the reddish-tinge made the world appear rosy. To Paul's dismay the dentist threw the battered brush straight into the bin. It was then that he met the colourful Donald with his red bow-tie, yellow bill and blue sailor's outfit.

In amongst the tatty and worn, it became his very own, *not to be touched* toothbrush. Alas, in no time at all, his duck brush also became shabby and dull. Paul's thirst for sucking cold water through the bristles whilst chewing on them didn't help. Nor the fact that everyone else ignored his request not to touch it. The enthusiasm to maintain a healthy set of white teeth eventually wore out, at about the same rate as the curling bristles. It is quite normal for one half-decent toothbrush to service the needs of the entire family, except, of course, for Paul's dad. On the advice of his dentist and in order to prevent future tooth decay, he'd had all his extracted when he was nineteen. Now he soaks them overnight in a glass of watered-down bleach.

The children, when they bother to clean their teeth, often use a minty powder. Needless to say, in the same way a communal tub of margarine becomes smeared with jam, mottled with toasted crumbs and a magnet for stray hairs, after a few dips of the brush the tin of powder becomes a feeky, clumpy, health risk. When the family is strapped for cash, salt is used. So Paul is delighted to see that here they use toothpaste, the one with the red and blue stripes.

Balancing his bundle of clothes in one hand, resembling a chimp hugging a big bunch of bananas, Paul uses his free hand to steady his ascent as he clambers up a steep and narrow staircase. The height of each carpeted step is more that he is used to. The ingrained rhythm of the stairs from home, traversed numerous times, can easily be scaled even in complete darkness. These, as plush as they seem, are unfamiliar and cause him to stumble, dropping his neatly-stacked garments. A hand from behind ensures he doesn't fall backwards and, for a half a moment, the double-decker bus to town rolls through his mind.

He enters a room in which two made-up single beds stand either side of a sash window. At the foot of each is a chest of drawers. The policeman tells Paul to place his clothes inside but to leave his pyjamas on the pillow, similar to the bed opposite. He hooks his gown alongside another larger one on the back of the door. The only other fixture is a cast iron radiator. Paul discovers it is scorching hot — such an extravagance considering the first tinge of autumn is yet to mar the September leaves. He is then taken back to the lounge and encouraged to go play with the kindergarten toys, but instead he chooses to read a book. In Green Class he had been making a concerted effort to progress with his reading before moving up to the juniors. Tomorrow the new school year begins. Bobby and Shane will be starting Class Four without him. Unable to concentrate he flips through the pages looking at the pictures, searching for one in particular: a hideous troll hiding underneath a footbridge.

The clanking of pans accompanies the aroma of cooked food. This reminds Paul's stomach, now rumbling in protest, that it hasn't been fed since breakfast. In the dining room Paul is glad to see Carole, who now resides in the girl's section, sitting at a large table with his brothers. Mark, the eldest, is also there. He was captured sneaking off home shortly after the family's arrival. Their father had given him the bus fare, telling him he could return home once he'd accompanied everyone to where they were going. Out of protest he folds his arms and declares he is on a hunger strike. Meanwhile, tucking into a sumptuous battered cod and chips, Darren chats about having a fight with the cock of the home, one of twins, who can be seen brooding at another table. Darren and Jason have usurped him. Paul can easily envisage Darren scrambling around scrapping with his lightning fists, whilst Jason makes sure neither his twin nor anyone else for that matter join in. The clash was all over in two minutes but the menacing atmosphere and whispers still continue.

Unlike Mark's hunger strike. Unable to resist the food, he craftily slits the underside and scoops out the fleshy white fish from inside its battered coat, then arranges his plate, minus a few chips, to look untouched. After eating, Carole and the girls go back to the female quarters and Paul joins the younger children to prepare for bed.

Paul's first night is a restless one. Reflective spectres continuously drift back and forth over the ceiling and walls. The sound of a metal drinks can being kicked across a pavement and the drone from a busy main road creates an unfamiliar sense of solitude. Fear of repercussions from his snoring room-mate, the other twin, also worry him. Come the light of day, Paul wakes relieved that the twin brother has stayed in his bed and is pleasantly surprised that his own bed has stayed dry.

Totally seduced by the warm novelties of wall-to-wall carpet and scrummy things, such as mini packets of breakfast cereal and fresh milk, Paul easily accepts this new regime. He sheds no tears and creates no tantrums.

Neither does he pine to return home or dwell on missing his father. There is no wondering why or where: events are just playing out.

Being separated from his siblings doesn't bother him either as he is able to wave to them at breakfast. His brothers sit at the boys' table, Carole at the girls' and Paul with the infants. Later that morning, when Paul joins the kindergarten class, nine-year-old Carole and Darren, although almost eleven, also attend the same class. Lessons consist of story-time on the carpet, melting cooking-chocolate to make cornflake cupcakes and playing with baby toys. Paul views it as a regression, backsliding to Yellow Class, whilst Carole and Darren seem delighted not to have to do any schoolwork. The children are free to join in or not, and as they are permitted to do whatever they want, they don't misbehave.

The routine of breakfast, kindergarten and bedtime glide smoothly along without upset to fuse the days. Time seems to fly. Awful tales told by his father about cruel whippings, malnutrition and forced labour, thankfully, never materialise. There are no sadistic nuns waddling about in Waybrook House seeking out victims to terrorise. Paul's father told them about the time he made the mistake of wincing as he rose to greet a priest visiting the orphanage. He was suffering from a condition called housemaid's knee, an inflammation on the kneecaps caused by spending long periods of time kneeling down and scrubbing the floors. The priest questioned the nuns about it, and subsequently Paul's father was accused of telling tales and beaten black and blue to teach him a lesson. A lesson, he says, he never forgot. There are no floor scrubbing chores to be done here. In fact, there are no chores at all and when Saturday rolls up he is even given pocket money. The younger children are escorted to a newsagent's to buy sweets. Paul purchases a packet of Rainbow Drops, multi-coloured grains of rice and puffed maize that resemble Rice Krispies. Fighting the urge to pour the packet directly into his mouth, he attempts to eat them one grain at a time. Paul relishes the sweet flavours of this new life of plenty. He expects more pocket money days will follow. He tilts back his head, tips the bag and gobbles the lot.

Perhaps the equilibrium of a misaligned universe suddenly rights itself, because the following day Paul is relocated to another orphanage. This move reunites the two little 'uns on the steps of Galilee House, an imposing three-storey red-brick building with a massive front door. A Victorian structure that appears as sinister and as foreboding as a debtor's prison. However, there are no gushing hugs and kisses. Instead the two exchange glances and gulp back fears as a black and white silhouette glides down the steps to receive them. Galilee House is a home for Catholic children and is managed by nuns. Clipped and direct, Sister Mary Grace greets the two with a tight smile that displays little emotion.

She directs the children to follow her. Their three elder brothers are nowhere in sight. Carole and Paul reach out for one another's hands. They enter a wide hallway. Echoes of the nun's hurried footsteps rebound off the stone floor, and the place smells of pine-disinfectant. On the third floor they are given a brief tour. Shown the bathroom, a laundry room, the kitchen and a day room, which contains a huge rocking horse. They pause outside the door of the Holy Mother Superior's office. In much the same fashion as the first home, the children are given clothing, only this time they are school uniforms which are green. The Holy Mother lays down the ground rules about order, no nonsense and cleanliness. When quizzed if either of them is a bed-wetter, Paul is quick to deny that he is. Carole, who normally possesses the inconvenient habit of blurting out the truth, says nothing.

Formalities over, they are shown to their rooms. Paul's is near the kitchen. A narrow space with a window. Close to the door is a single bed and a wardrobe. Placed back-to-back to make a room partition, a second wardrobe and bed mirrors the first. Paul is pointed towards the one by the window and told to make himself at home while Carole and Sister Grace continue on down the corridor. The bed nearest the door has a neatly folded nightie on its pillow and a pair of pink slippers on the floor. The one nearest the window already has orange pyjamas on its pillow. Paul's plimsolls are tucked just beneath the bed. The wardrobe stands open and, recognising items of clothing acquired from the previous place, Paul deposits his uniform there. Through the window Paul spies grey clouds and an empty playground. Then Carole reappears with the nun who takes them back to the day room before leaving the two alone.

"Do you like it?" Paul, who's yet to make up his mind, needs a second opinion.

"Naw, do you?"

"Naw, it's horrible. Do you think they're gonna smack us." It is a legitimate enquiry if, like Paul, you are prone to bouts of naughtiness.

"Maybe they won't, if we'm extra good."

Paul doesn't rate his chances.

A moment of silence passes, their vision drawn towards a painted pony with flared nostrils and glaring eyes. It remains motionless as though tethered, awaiting its rider. Large enough to seat an adult, it is such an impressive beast. Temptation momentarily wipes away concern as the two exchange *shall we* glances. A naughty glint in Carole's eyes triggers Paul's impulse to be the first. They both bolt over, unable to resist mounting the steed. Astride with Paul holding tightly on to the reins and Carole gripping him by the waist, they rock back and forth in a galloping motion. Whee-wor! Whee-wor! Whee-wor! Upon creaky metal springs the thing creates one horrendous din and Sister Mary Grace comes rushing in.

"Off!" she commands. "It's Sunday."

They quickly dismount, half expecting a clip around the ear but instead they receive a warning.

"You had better learn the rules. We show respect on the Lord's day."

Such a pompous tone would normally have the two biting their fists to suppress laughter, but not on this occasion.

Early the next morning, after a deep sleep, Paul wakes up in a wet bed. He chastises himself with some choice insults. He didn't wet the bed once at Waybrook and was beginning to believe that, perhaps, he had grown out of it. Peeping around the side of the wardrobe, the lumpy outline of his room-mate rises and falls in a slumberous rhythm. Sleeping soundly is a girl whose appearance is more akin to a grown-up than a child. Paul hasn't been introduced and fears she may be a nun. He silently removes his wet pyjama bottoms and pops on his dressing-gown. He then peels back the bed covers. A large damp patch shows, so as noiselessly as he can Paul removes the bottom sheet and flips over the mattress. Using the top sheet as a bottom one, he covers up his offence by remaking the bed. He bundles the pyjama trousers up with the wet sheet before looking about for a place to stash the evidence. Carrying his bundle he sidles by the sleeping girl. Over the cabbagey aroma of damp urine his nostrils detect a hint of bottled scent. He concludes that nuns don't wear perfume, and so therefore she isn't one, and quietly exits the room. The hallway is deserted. Barefooted, the cold stone floor keeps him on his toes as he makes his way quickly down the corridor to the laundry room. He has the notion to wash the bundle before anyone can discover his misdeed. Not exactly a foolproof plan considering he hasn't a clue how to use a washing machine. The door is locked. Flummoxed about what to do next and not knowing where Carole sleeps, he heads to the bathroom praying he'll bump into her there. That too is deserted so he dumps the sheet into a waiting laundry basket and returns to his room where he places his pyjama bottoms on the radiator.

At breakfast Carole and Paul sit at a table with three other children, all girls and all in their teens. They appear uninterested in the two newcomers. Sister Mary Agatha, a robust cook with thick arms, rounds the table and with a swift heavy flick, deftly deposits a dollop of porridge into the bottom of each waiting bowl.

The girls bow their heads as Sister Agatha begins to say grace. "For what we are about to receive, may the Lord..."

Paul wisely suppresses *"Please, save us,"* a comical interjection that doesn't seem all that funny, this morning.

"Amen!" the table chants. Hands quickly touch base with forehead, navel and shoulders, then spoons dive in. Paul much prefers porridge the way his father makes it using both sugar and salt with a ring of cold milk, to chill the edges. This grey mush clinging to his spoon appears to contain neither. Resigned to the stodge, the three girls gobble it down as though half starved. But viewing their furrowed brows it seems that none of them are enjoying it, and the girl who looks the most unhappy Paul recognises as his room-mate.

Sister Grace enters the day room. Casting an ominous shadow over the table, she looms before all like a drill sergeant. Straight-backed, chin up, suspicious eyes both accusing and challenging at the same time. Paul is familiar with this stern expression. He braces himself.

"Where is your bed linen?"

"I took it off 'cause I was too hot." Paul thinks this fib sounds plausible.

"And these?" She dangles his orange pyjama bottoms, which are dry but smell like ammonia.

"Erm..." His blushes deepen. He hears "He wet the bed" whispered by his room-mate.

"Follow me!"

She tells Paul to fetch his sheets and then takes him to the laundry room, where he is instructed to place them inside the washing machine. Sister Grace shows him how much soap powder to add and which settings to use. He is to return after mass to peg the sheets upon the line. Next time he is to wash and hang his own soiled bedding. Then he is returned, for the sake of starving children in Africa, to finish every last speck of his porridge. He receives no thrashing, which is a pleasant surprise although throughout the whole of morning mass he frets, half expecting further admonishment. Miraculously the following night and all those thereafter, Paul remains dry.

He attends a local Catholic school which is a short walk around the corner. Never the brightest academically, he finds, perhaps because he is the oldest in the class, that he can manage the lessons. Unfortunately he's been assigned to the wrong class and is soon moved up into the juniors. Here he becomes the youngest student and understands nothing. He is made to sit at the front, where he is assessed by failing to answer a single question correctly. In the playground, under grey skies he stands alone. No child wants to play with the new boy, orphan Paul. It is now that he pines to go home.

When Pocket Money Day arrives, the nuns tell the children there will be none. Carole and Paul are terribly disappointed. The money is being saved to pay for the orphans' summer holidays, which are a long way off as it is barely mid-September. Instead of visiting the sweetshop they are permitted to play outside within the grounds of Galilee House.

Children from another section of the home are also out and about but there is still no sign of their elder brothers. Carole and Paul clamber around the metal climbing frame. The seesaw becomes vacant so Paul rushes to it but Carole misses her opportunity to join him when a boy of about ten years old occupies the opposite end. Seesawing away, Paul relishes the interaction with a kid other than his sister. Until said kid waits until Paul is at the highest point before purposely slipping back off the edge of his seat. Whoosh, smack, ouch, the seesaw crashes down sending a jolt through Paul's bones and scraping his ankle. He yelps in pain but it is the sudden shock that really makes him weep. The boy runs away laughing and a concerned Carole steps up to mother her little brother.

Chapter Seventeen: Normality Returns

Carole and Paul sit folding and arranging clothes. They have been back home for just under five minutes. Immediately upon their return, as though nothing untoward ever happened and determined that life should get back to normal as quickly as possible, their dad sent them straight upstairs to Carole's room to continue the garment-sorting chore they had left scattered about the floor. A mixture of loneliness and guilt brought about this change of circumstance. Given the *moment of peace* that he so often implored of them, it turned out Paul's father couldn't bear the silence. He then requested the children be returned. Carole and Paul are both overjoyed and view the whole episode like a holiday. They even get to keep their new possessions.

"Rags, rags, rags, keep, rags, rags, rags." Sorting with speed, the mound of clothes melts away like snow in the rain. Paul is desperate to play out and, more importantly, to show off his new snake-belt. In the street he makes sure to display it to Crybaby Kenny who acknowledges it by asking Paul to his birthday party, which is *a first*. Paul has often watched classmates hand out party invitations on fancy writing paper with matching envelopes. So-and-so is having a birthday party at such-and-such a place, on this or that date: please tick the box if you can attend. Paul often pretends not to notice, making out he isn't bothered when the deliverers continually pass him by. Though he doesn't have it in writing he is proud to be asked to someone's birthday party. He runs back into the house. Overjoyed he sings out to Carole and his father, "Kenny Cropper says I can go to his birfdy parrrty," his smile stretching as wide as his teeth will allow.

"Don't believe everything you hear." This curt response thumb-squishes his glee like a bothersome flea.

"No, really, he said I could." Paul's head nodding assurance convinces Carole but not his dad.

"Well, just don't count ya chickens, then you won't be disappointed, will ya?"

Having a pragmatist for a father often frustrates Paul. Especially when he is correct. Street politics will not allow certain children to play with others, and the same goes for party invitations. Within the hour, Kenny rescinds his invite. His mother said no, so Paul becomes uninvited. In response Paul tells him that he won't be getting the Scalextric racing-set he was going to give him for a birthday present. Kenny's eyes pop and his chin drops. To further bolster Paul's ridiculous claim, he runs back home to search the cubby-hole under the stairs. He returns holding a blue hand-throttle from a long-gone race track that Mark once owned. Squeezing its plastic plunger numerous times produces a springy sound, demonstrating just how exciting the gift would have been. Crybaby Kenny immediately decides that Paul *can* come his party after all. He implores him to attend. Paul says no and even if it is all a fallacy, for a brief moment he feels superior to possess something that somebody else wants.

Paul doesn't tell his new teacher Mr Barnes or any of his classmates that he has been in a children's home. Strangely, neither Bobby nor Shane questions his absence. If asked, he's already decided to lie. Carole told him to say he'd been on holiday, to Birmingham, which wasn't all that far from the truth. Paul simply slots back into place, rejoining his class, which has moved up from the infants to the juniors. Trading in the small playground with its climbing frame, sandpit and aviary, for a huge one with a sports field and an *out-of-bounds* grass bank: *the Ditch,* hidden away in the corner out of sight from teachers on playground duty. It's where daredevil pupils nonchalantly stroll by, then suddenly vanish as they dive down it like a commando. Mostly the kids roll down the slope but the real thrill comes from spying over the top, waiting for the right moment to re-emerge. Trying not to get caught when rushing out to blend in with the children playing nearby.

Though it isn't raining, the grass is still deemed too wet to use. The boys from Paul's class dash around the tarmacked playground chasing after a tennis ball which they use to play footy. The girls, playing a horse-themed game, jump and bray. Paul isn't up for playing with the boys so instead he chooses to canter alongside whichever girls neigh back at him. On this particular occasion someone bellows "Kiss chase!" Repeated numerous times, the words become a chant and suddenly chaos ensues as the opposing troops mix to play. This popularity contest has some girls skipping merrily, lacking any real effort to get away, whilst others dart about screeching in absolute terror. Paul's initial enthusiasm evokes the latter and he receives a kick in the shins in place of a kiss. Only Jenny Merrill, a rank outsider often ostracised from the herd because they say she smells like piss, allows Paul to capture her. Obviously, as life often shows, it is the fittest runners that catch the prettiest girls, and as quickly as the game erupts so does it simmer down. A few moments before the end-of-play whistle, Jenny asks Paul if he wants to be her boyfriend. It isn't her bright personality and winning smile that persuades him to accept. In truth she hardly ever smiles and her disposition is generally somewhat glum. Paul agrees on the proviso that their relationship remains a secret. He further negotiates the receipt of a rubber bouncy ball and two pencil-men. Schoolyard currency, these fruit 'n' veg characters with facial features and protruding limbs fit on the top of pencils. Paul prefers the banana man because he wears a red cowboy hat and isn't covered in teeth marks, unlike the orange one which has also lost both of its arms. Jenny seems satisfied with this arrangement and lavishes him with further tokens of affection, gifting him sweets and other pencil-case related articles. Despite being an almost perfect match, they only kiss the once, and their affair doesn't last the day. Jenny gets into serious trouble when, for the second time, she is caught red-handed stealing from pockets and pump-bags in the cloakroom. All her booty, including Paul's horde, gets confiscated thus dissolving their romantic arrangement.

It takes a week or thereabouts for Paul to properly settle back into school life; to detach himself from the relative calmness that surrounds the girls and to jump back into the chaos of boisterous play with Bobby and Shane. Their gang, the Anti-Creeps, gets rebranded to a new group called the Social Scroungers. Shane and Bobby, the two best fighters in class, have joined Paul in announcing the receipt of free school-dinners. With backup such as this, Paul now wears the once humiliating badge with a sense of pride.

Perhaps pride is a bit strong. What becomes clear is that Paul is in good company and is no longer the only child on benefits. Seen by those in the know, the signs of which families receive welfare assistance is evident. Matching clothes in exchange for a welfare voucher, certain styles, cuts and fabrics worn by the poorer children. Trousers, shirts and, the biggest give away of all, duffle coats. There is some choice: end of range shoes are often included in what can be selected. It just so happens that Bobby has chosen the exact same pair as Paul. Hickory-brown lace-ups decorated with interweaved leatherette strips of dark green and burgundy. Fashioned in the seventies, they are bulky with hard wooden platform-heels that clack as they walk. Bobby and Paul obtain some Blakey's Segs, metal shoe sole protectors, which they hammer into the heels. This transforms their clack into a click, making their footfalls even louder. Crouching, knees bent as though balancing on an invisible surfboard, they get two speedy mates to pull them along. Feet set firmly in place, they grind and scrape over the hard surface of the playground making a horrendous racket, not unlike a jet engine, and leaving a trail of sparks flickering behind them. The heat produced is something to marvel at and they trick Mr Brown, who is supervising break-time, into touching them. Gentle Mr Brown with his half-moon glasses and wispy clown hair, a favourite teacher to many pupils, yowls, kisses his fingers and flaps them about. He takes it in good humour, calling them naughty scallywags and adding how Carole, who often walks beside him at playtime, is always such a well-mannered child. Paul feels a tiny tinge of remorse for pranking such a nice teacher and hopes that Carole doesn't let slip at home what he's done to his new shoes. When at school Carole rarely interacts with Paul. Her father has ordered her, after numerous complaints of embarrassment by Darren, to leave her brothers alone. In her early schooldays she'd follow Darren around the playground pleading with him to play with her.

In class Paul attempts to catch up with his reading. His fellow students appear to be tearing through the rainbow: red and yellow, blue, orange and green, indigo, violet and rainbow. For those extra bright students, there even follow silver and gold reading books. Paul begins the green series which contains fewer pictures making understanding the story a good deal more difficult. And with the smaller text come larger words and longer sentences. These lengthy typescript paragraphs blur and shake, making it impossible for Paul's weary eyes to hold position. Forcefully gritting his teeth whilst rapidly vibrating his skull does nothing to help him focus, neither does clasping his face, hair pulling or eye gouging. Frustratingly he recites one word at a time and staggers to the end of each line but it makes no sense without a drawing to guide the story. Paul just can't remember the words he's already read, and more often than not he begins to re-read the same line over and over. Paul much prefers being read to but that no longer happens in the junior classes.

At home-time Carole waits by the school gate so she and Paul can walk together. They cut through the car-park behind the nearby shops. Taking a mini detour they head over to one specific corner, a breezy corner where sweet wrappers twist alongside spirals of leaves. Beside the tall bins stowed there, they have a quick scout around for any discarded objects worth salvaging. Empty-handed this time they head towards the high-rise flats where the blustery wind whirls with such force the children are able to fly. Paul opens his duffle coat, pulls up his hood and tucks both hands into his pockets to create wings. He then leaps from a wall. Out of control, Paul is carried by a gust so strong that he is lifted up higher than he has ever been lifted before. It unnerves him and he instantly collapses his wings; coat flapping loosely he braces for impact. Luckily, and with a huge sigh of relief, Paul touches down upon the soft grass just missing the hard pathway. He postpones any further flights for another day.

Paul chases to catch up with Carole. Despite it being a mild day, he can see she is rushing towards the high-rise alcove for a blast of warm laundry air. As a matter of course, they barge and battle for the prime location directly beneath the vent. Their father has instructed them to come straight home after school without dawdling, so knowing that he is watching the clock they don't linger for long. They routinely stop, though just for a moment, to drool over their imagination, gawping through the window of the bakery at the delicious jam tarts and chocolate eclairs.

Today Providence decrees they are due a treat. The cake-lady taps on the window beckoning them inside. She offers them both a free iced-bun. Sticky and sweet, it is indeed a treat, one that they speedily accept with nods of beaming thanks. Worried they may have dawdled too slowly, they munch and step up the pace. Carole suggests they nip into the greengrocer's to see if they have any loose cabbage leaves. Finely shredded their dad feeds them to his pigeons. Then they pop next-door to the butcher's to ask if he has any bones for the dog. Bearing such gifts should explain, if required, why the journey home took more than the allotted twenty minutes. Their father is pleased to receive the cabbage leaves and, with a fleshy bone to gnaw, Red gives thanks with a raised paw.

As their school uniforms are still very new, they are sent upstairs to change before eating tea. Bread and jam, what else? Avoiding the crumbs and unwelcome particles, Paul deftly excavates a clean layer of margarine to spread on his bread. With less attention he slathers jam over both pieces and slaps them together. He doesn't sit to eat. Clamping his sandwich in his mouth, he puts on his duffle coat and rushes out to play.

Although Guy Fawkes is many weeks away, in the back garden a huge pyramid of branches, wood and other flammable objects is beginning to take shape. November the fifth is Bonfire Night. Paul's passion for flames flickers much brighter at this time of year. He and his brothers actually began collecting firewood at the end of August just prior to their children's home vacation. With the permission of its owner, the large, climbable tree two gardens away supplies many of the branches. It is this tree in which the brothers leap from branch to branch whilst playing parachute commandos. Thinning it out to increase their fun they remove the awkward limbs and flimsy side shoots, leaving alone the strong and springy. They also leave behind a bedraggled tree that looks like their own messy hair of a morning. The bonfire as it stands is almost one storey high and will surely get a lot thicker and much taller before the fifth arrives.

Paul heads off in search of more burnables. Through a gate in the back alleyway he enters the rear garden of number thirty-seven. The house is unoccupied but he is still careful not to be discovered. The Wrights live right next door. Their fence is a high view-blocking one but not if they happen to gaze from an upstairs window. Luckily they don't own a dog to sniff him out and alert them with a bark, otherwise he wouldn't have braved it. Paul spies a white enamel sink amongst a pile of weeds and debris. He can see it is made of metal and has a draining board but no taps. His mind turns from wood collecting to salvaging, all thoughts of discovery vanquished in an instant. He pulls. The vessel, weighed down by rubbish and entwined within the thorny grasp of brambles, hardly budges. Paul struggles to free the sink. Scraping on stone, clanking on wood he lifts, rattles, heaves and drops. Through sheer determination he manages to yank the sink loose. Metal grating on paving slabs, he hauls it out of the garden and drags it down the alleyway. Heads pop over fences to see who is making such a din, but they're too late voicing their annoyance as Paul closes his garden gate. Tomorrow he will use the sink to make a small pond ready for the spring when he'll begin a new hunt for frogs.

October is over; Halloween passed by with little more than a mention. Bonfire Night has arrived. Carole and Paul create a Guy Fawkes effigy: an old pair of trousers and a jumper stuffed with newspaper. Carole uses her sewing skills to stitch the legs to the body and they tie knots at the open ends of the garments to secure the insides. A paper bag with scrawled features makes up the head. As they will be pushing the Guy around in a shopping trolley they decide there is no need for shoes. And as neither one of them has ever seen a Guy with hands, they don't bother with those either. The children shout "Penny for the guy!" as they steer down the main road, heading to the shops. They hope to make enough money to purchase some fireworks. This olden day tradition peaked years ago and they find that people are less inclined to part with their cash. A grand total of twenty-seven and a half pence is all they collect. So they buy some sweets instead.

As predicted, come the fifth the bonfire has grown, mostly in width thanks to a sofa, a stained mattress and a myriad of other household combustibles retrieved from a derelict site. At the very top Mark has balanced a wooden chair upon which slumps a forlorn Guy. Paul has checked, as instructed by the television presenters on Blue Peter, that no hedgehogs have wandered in for a sleep. Red, who is totally unfazed by thunderclaps and lightning flashes, is shut inside the downstairs toilet out of harm's way.

The family gathers around. Damp and cold, it isn't easy for the flames to take hold. Eventually, at the expense of his eyebrows, Jason manages to get it started. A splash of paraffin, a bright explosion and voilà, in a flash it is roaring like an angry dragon. An angry dragon set ablaze. Glowing with joy, orange faces stare out. A skyward jet of sparks emits a sprinkle of glitter. The evening, a little overcast, is holding back on the rain. They hear bangs and squeals, their flashes hidden from view. It's getting difficult to see much beyond the colossal tongue of the burning beast. The heat forces them back a couple of metres, and then further still as it intensifies. Eventually they reverse up the stone-covered ramp to stand at the side of the house. By the time the hot-dogs are ready, they are near to the back door. Lovingly prepared in the kitchen, their father serves them up with slightly burnt onions and tomato ketchup. Paul knows from the glows that there are plenty of other fires burning in the vicinity. He guesses that not many are as big, or as hot, as theirs.

This year their dad appears a little more enthusiastic than usual. Fireworks are a big waste of money, as far as he's concerned, so it comes as a pleasant surprise when he produces a packet of sparklers. Silver circles of crackling sprinkles entertain the children. Scrawling names that linger no longer than the briefest moment. Before they putter, Darren and Jason hurl theirs across the garden. Chasing after them, they throw them once more up into the air, Jason scorches his fingers and everybody laughs. Making this the best bonfire night ever, there's another surprise: drinking chocolate poured into mugs and carried outside on a tray. The delight on everyone's face reflects in their father's eyes.

It seems that all darkness has been vanquished for the night. Then suddenly a loud bang comes from the kitchen. The baking potatoes have exploded in the oven. The door, already defective, blows right off the hinges and so ends its life. It's a new problem that their father says will have to wait for the morning.

The fire continues to blaze for many hours. The washing line melts and, yet to be discovered, a blackened side of the house.

Chapter Eighteen: Going Underground

"They've got kids," Carole jubilantly calls out.

Paul rushes over to join her at the front room window. Heaving himself onto the windowsill is a strain. In the struggle his protruding tongue accidentally strokes the tobacco-stained net curtains. "Eww yuck..." He splutters and licks his sleeve but the dry fabric makes him cringe and wish that he hadn't.

In the procession of dark-haired children toing and froing between battered car and front door, Paul spies a stroppy, duffle-coated youth carrying a box.

"Yeahhh," he cheers, "one of them's my age."

"There's loads of girls," Carole adds.

Her observation sparks interest from the three eldest. Now, all five children are peering through the grubby net curtains.

A new family, the Lofts, are moving into the cul-de-sac at number thirty-seven. To get a clearer view Paul lifts the net curtain and dips underneath, letting it fall behind him. This movement draws the attention of one of the girls. Embarrassed, the three eldest instantly duck out of sight before scurrying back to their game of cards. The Loft family has eight children, of which six are girls. Unfortunately they all appear either too small or too tall to play with Carole. The bigger boy looks to be about the right age to hang out with Darren and the littler one, Paul was quick to notice, has the potential, height-wise, to be a new friend of his.

Initial encounters don't go smoothly. On the first day together Darren and the elder boy, Stephen Loft, trade blows over a penknife. Younger siblings Clive and Paul dance about, each cheering their own battling brother. Darren grips Stephen in a headlock, pausing long enough to notice the two annoying younger brothers.

The fight ends with Clive and Paul being chased off up the street. Stephen whacks Clive around the head and Darren gives Paul a dead-leg punch. United by a universal aversion to bratty brothers and with the pecking order firmly established, Darren and Stephen instantly become best buddies. Having a common enemy also bonds the young 'uns. When looking for a playmate, Paul now opts to try his luck with the new kid a mere pebble flick away. Door numbering as it is, one side even and the other odd, conveniently places thirty-seven in the circle at the bottom of Paul's road exactly four houses away from number forty-six.

Clive, who is always wearing his duffle coat, has a tendency to exude spit bubbles whilst talking. He is a year younger than eight-year-old Paul. His household of ten appears chaotic and somewhat rowdy whenever Paul calls around. Most times Clive is available to play. If ever his mom forbids him, he climbs out an upstairs window and shimmies down the drainpipe. When she chastises him, he often answers back with an outburst of profanity. Threats of receiving a beating from his strict father, a huge terrifying man, seem to have no effect. Still, linked by that common irk, banishment by big brothers, they become a unit and it is not long before both of them are chasing, following and, whenever possible, spying on their brothers.

Shortly after Clive's family move into the street they are invited to join the tenants' association. They attend one meeting. Paul's family are at the top of the agenda. They discuss getting up a petition to have the nuisance household evicted. News of this reaches his dad via Mr Loft whilst supping a pint of ale at his local. Back home, everyone can hear their father is furious as he complains to Bill, exclaiming, "They're all *bloody* idiots!" to the neighbours on the other side of the dining-room wall.

The notion of being thrown out does play a little on Paul's mind, as it must do with his other siblings. One dark evening, donning a disguise of a hefty overcoat, some thick-rimmed glasses and a musty grey wig he found in an empty house, an audacious Jason holding a clipboard knocks at Mrs Chadwick's door. Displaying his mock petition, one badly worded but cleverly typed on a ribbon-less typewriter using a sheet of blue carbon paper, he asks in a crotchety voice if her husband would like to sign the petition. "I'll just get my pen," he says, heading back to retrieve one. Then his wife's booming voice hollers, "It's those fools from next door." Erupting with laughter the hidden spectators mockingly reveal themselves. Mrs Chadwick slams the door and they hear loud quarrelling coming from the other side. Paul's dad, who often quotes the proverb "Live and let live," says that he does not normally condone such mischievous behaviour but admits it was rather amusing.

After overhearing their brothers mention Windsor Park, Clive and Paul deliberate whether to follow. Hoping not to be seen, they flit between gateposts and deftly weave their way up the road in the shadow of parked cars. They crouch behind dustbins and squash themselves, often with urgency, behind wooden telegraph poles. Clive gets a big splinter in the webbing of his thumb. Paul plucks it out, impressed that he manages it so easily and doubly amazed at Clive's unflinching bravery.

From a distance they wait and watch as the four figures of Mark, Jason, Darren and Stephen cross the open fields. Only when they vanish down the banks of the brook do Clive and Paul break cover from the dark side of a wall. Keeping close to the shrubbery, avoiding open spaces, they jog down the vacant path leading to the stream. The sloping sides are compact and not sludgy. It hasn't rained recently so the water runs shallow. This allows them, by hopping back and forth over the snaking flow, to tread mainly on dry ground.

There are a few dodgy sections. Dark, overgrown canopies that steal away the light and sharp, low-hanging brambles that tangle hair. Segments where the water spreads wide at certain flat points or gathers in deep pools, where caution is required to reach the other side. Paul forgets to warn Clive about the green mossy boulder and, sure enough, his foot also glides on contact. Only when Clive loses balance *both* feet splash down, soaking his trousers to just below his knees. Crybaby Kenny would have run home squealing but not Clive: he simply squeezes out what he can and squishes on. To keep up with their brothers they have to climb out of the brook to run along the bank. Occasionally, like soldiers under fire, they hit the deck or dive back down the bank out of sight. Never once do their brothers look back and so remain blissfully unaware they are being tracked.

At the end of the park they reach the start of the channel, the beginning of the water source. It is a conduit for rain water and the occasional overflow of sewage, a drainage tunnel leading beneath the road. The entrance is obstructed by iron railings. The bars, slightly warped, allow skinny kids to squeeze through thus gaining access to the subterranean blackness. Clive and Paul peer inside the darkened mouth cautiously. Footfalls and excited talk resound to the accompaniment of bobbing torchlight bouncing around the tubular walls. In silent agreement the pursuers effortlessly slip through the bars and, although they can stand without bumping their heads, find it slow going to walk on a tunnel floor so curved. Plodding on with one foot either side of the flow, they waddle forward like cowboys who have ridden for days. Up ahead their brothers turn a corner; the dancing light, their point of focus, fades. Behind, the shrinking entrance resembles a silver moon in a starless sky. Selfishly it shares none of its illumination this far along the passage. Clive and Paul are swallowed by the blackness. Reaching out, Paul grabs hold of Clive's sleeve and Clive does the same. Supporting each other they continue, with trepidation, into the unknown, Paul's claustrophobia held at bay by Clive's bravado and the knowledge their brothers are but a goose-honk away should they get lost in the dark. This loud guttural blast, emitted with power, cuts through trees and over houses and can be heard from very far away. It has become a signal used to locate one another when out and about.

The pace lagging, time and distance is warped by the stretches of darkness. Deprived of sight, it is not their ears that compensate but their noses. The distorted reverberations of man and machine above them become a rippled drone, the smell of green algae more prevalent. When the two round the corner the torchlight, a faint halo, completely vanishes leaving behind a smidgen of hazy grey. As they approach, the tunnel opens into a cavern. The haze reveals itself to be thin shards of daylight and, to Paul's delight, a haven delivering fresh air. Set into the wall, a ladder of steel steps leads up to a manhole cover. The wheels of a motorcar passing over rattles them. A timely warning of what dangers await should they be foolish enough to climb up.

Further on, a slimy waterfall ramp impedes their progress. It isn't particularly steep nor is it long, but with nothing to cling on to the slippery surface makes it difficult to clamber up it. After four slow and careful attempts, it is Clive who discovers that running straight up is the best way to succeed. Paul also manages to tackle the ramp, with a well-timed helping hand from Clive. The next section of the tunnel is not so high, and for a short, indeterminable distance crouching is necessary. It reaches a second dog-leg junction before opening out into a larger pipe as before. In front there is no sign of their brothers but, growing with each step, is a disc of daylight.

Beneath a blue sky, Clive and Paul exit the dark, circular tunnel to enter a square, open channel. With tall concrete walls, minus the green slime sides, it is much like a canal lock. Too high for the children to climb out alone, but perhaps with a bunk up it will be possible. They hear the rush of many cars driving past on a nearby main road. Continuing their tracking, they follow the fresh splashes and the occasional footprints that mark the dry edges of the gully. They scurry past back gardens. Jumping up they see the fences and green hedges, chimneys too.

A bridge built over the watercourse slightly hinders their progress. A metre-high slot stretching out the width and length of a road faces them. This forces the pair to squat-walk like Sumo wrestlers to advance. Any worries about wet feet are put aside because Paul has to avoid dipping his bum in the water and, at the same time, try not to disturb the spider nests above his head. Once through they run to make up for lost time.

Reaching a second tunnel mouth, this one without any bars, Clive and Paul continue their adventure by returning into the bowels of the earth. This time there is no torchlight to guide and no voices to encourage. Still, Clive and Paul brave the dark once more. They travel in a straight line and, when the entrance glow fades, they question whether to continue. Curiosity pulls them on until they reach a well of daylight illuminating a junction. Two smaller tunnels split left and right. As they will have to crouch-walk to go along those, they decide to climb the horseshoe steps to a manhole above. Cautiously lifting the web-plastered lid, they see greenery. Clive shoves away the cover, his head popping up next to a rancid compost bin. There is no sign of their brothers. They recognise the collection of vegetable patches and tool sheds to be garden allotments, inner-city green spaces rented out to green-thumbed enthusiasts. They rush out of the hole, hastily pull up some carrots and snap a couple of rhubarb stalks. Then, like *pesky wabbits*, vanish back down into their underground warren. Scurrying through the tunnel they reverse the way they've come, deciding to head towards home. They have to scuttle back under the awkward road bridge, but rather than traipse blindly through their subterranean route, they scramble up the high wall of the open channel to join a footpath leading them once again into the playing fields of Windsor Park.

After re-entering the park, Paul suggests they dip back into the brook to have a quick search for frogs. Clive says that he wants to play on the giant slide and rushes off to climb the ladder. Paul, waiting at the bottom, has an offer. A bribe to reveal the secret location of his primo hunting ground: the cascading ledge. Clive is convinced and, in the leisurely blink of a frog's eye, their shadows once more darken the banks. They rummage about the edges, looking under grass clumps. Suddenly a frog hops out from the shade of a fern. Swift to react, the boys' hands, hampered by rhubarb and carrots, collide allowing the frog to land on the soft silt right near the water's edge. Paul is quick to release his goodies. He swoops, catching hold. It is a slippery little thing and slides from his grasp like a bar of wet soap. Flicking its legs, nose pointing downwards, it vanishes into the fizzing foam of the waterfall. Clive removes his shoes and socks, stuffing them into his coat pockets. He rolls up his damp trouser legs and pushes back a sleeve. Standing in the pool he uses a stalk of rhubarb to scare the frog, which is hiding beneath the ledge. There's a lot of splashing and laughing before Paul recaptures the green amphibian.

Now, with carrots and rhubarb protruding from his back pocket, he carries the frightened frog within cupped hands. In protest it squirms about. Paul can see froggy nostrils through a small space between his thumbs. The poor creature, pushing with all its might, attempts to prise open the gap. It does a wee. Paul isn't fazed; he's determined to release it into his own pond at home. The white metal sink he'd found in Clive's back garden, sunk into the ground, sits in front of the pigeon pen. His dad considered using it as a bathtub for his racing birds but Paul beat him to it by collecting frogspawn in the spring. The hatched tadpoles have now grown front limbs and are developing well. To help them along, Paul tied a bit of bacon-rind to a piece of shoelace, attached it to a stick and balanced it across the middle of the sink. Dangling in the water, the greedy wigglers couldn't get enough of it.

As Red never allows anyone who isn't family into his domain, Clive and Paul part company in the back alley. On the top step, near the back door, Paul admires his frog. Red pulls taut his chain, sniffing the air in a curious manner. Allowing Red to smell what is concealed in his cupped hands, Paul recites a rhyme. "Frogs smile, toads frown, they hop in the air not crawl on the ground." Interested to see more, the dog claws at Paul's hands making him release it. His jaws snap to catch the falling frog. Paul reacts quickly, yelling, "LEAVE!" This momentary distraction allows the lucky frog to hop safely away. Paul recaptures it as it heads down the steps and, satisfied it is unharmed, places it into the pond. He watches the tadpoles scatter as the frog dives, disturbing the muddy bottom. Waiting for the murk to settle, Paul breaks off the end of his rhubarb stalk and proceeds to strip back the stringy outer layer. Pursed lips contort his face and he blinks as he sucks the juice from the sour fibres. It isn't pleasant. He nips into the house and, although he knows he'll get a smack if he's caught, dips the chewed end of his rhubarb into the sugar bowl and munches on it. He does this a couple of times. Out in the street, Clive is sitting on his own front wall with a cup of sugar doing exactly the same.

***

It's one of those lazy, sunny days when everyone is playing outside. 'Bohemian Rhapsody' pours from a loudspeaker poking out of a window at number thirty-three. Charley's longhaired older brother, Alan, and his girlfriend stand intimately close, puffing on cigarettes whilst chatting to Kenny Cropper's big brother, Peter. Outside number thirty-five Mr Wright tinkers beneath a car bonnet on his driveway. There are lots of children darting about. Kenny Cropper stands facing a lamppost: it looks as if he's crying but he isn't. Instead he's counting loudly. Martin Murphy from Paul's school and Ginger Charley are amongst the children that run away to hide. Further up the street, Paul spies Carole playing gutters with Kenny's sister, Mandy. Standing on the pavement at opposite sides of the road, they take turns throwing a large football, attempting to hit the kerb. When it strikes the kerb the thrower scores a point and gets to throw again. If the thrower catches the ball before it touches the ground, they score two points, but not if the other player catches it, then it becomes their turn. The rules are simple. Both players must remain on the pavement until the ball is thrown, and when one player reaches ten points, they swap sides. The first to twenty is the winner. Paul finds it best to play against kids his own size as the bigger kids always reach twenty before he's sufficiently warmed up.

"Can I play the winner?" Paul asks, as he approaches with Clive in tow.

"You'll have to wait your turn, I'm next," Debbie Murphy righteously interjects.

"Then it's me!" adds Pamela, removing her lollipop just long enough to speak. Paul notices Pamela and her twin brother from the grove always have lots of sweets.

"No, you ay, I'm after Debbie," demands Glen, her twin.

"It's my ball," Mandy reminds everyone. "So, first it's Debbie, then it is Glen, then Pamela, then Paul and then it's Clive."

Paul takes a seat on the wall joining the queue. A queue that vanishes the instant the chimes of the ice-cream van sound. *Ding-dong, ding-dong, your nose is this long.* Like lifting up a plant-pot, all living creatures, except Carole and Paul, scuttle off to their houses calling out, "The I scream man's 'ere." The ball bounces before rolling in the gutter.

Watching and waiting until all purchases have been concluded, Carole and Paul stand to one side. Paul checks out the colourful advertisements stuck to the window of the serving-hatch. If he did have money he'd struggle to choose between the Zoom rocket and the Fab ice-lolly with its chocolate top and coloured sprinkles. Andy, the ice-cream man, is well aware of what the pair want. Using all the manners they possess, they ask, "Excuse me please, 'ave ya got any broken cornets... thank you very much?" Nine times out of ten they do get some, so they know it is worth the wait.

The children don't always go without sweets and ice-creams. There is always Christmas and Mrs McGaveridge on Saturday, and, every April, they have a visit from Mrs Hodges. Last April, the children were allowed to keep the birthday money she brought for Carole and her brothers. Paul cannot forget it. His fifty pence piece was a special one with a circle of nine clasping hands. Unfortunately he never got to buy any ice-cream. Red had been barking, as he so often did, and Paul's dad had shouted, to no one in particular, "Go and check what the dog's barking at!" So Paul ran to look over the fence at the bottom of the garden. Prior to checking, he placed his coin under a small, flat stone for safe-keeping. Alas, when he returned he couldn't find it. Paul began to question the location and lifted many similar-shaped stones, but all to no avail. He dug around for days searching for his lost treasure, leaving a wide crater in the centre of what had been a freshly-raked vegetable patch ready for sowing. On several occasions since he has returned to the search. He suspects that one of his brothers may have taken it, but, as he is unsure, he searches anyway.

Chapter Nineteen: There For The Taking

Carole and Paul are treading dirty washing in the bath. It is an arduous chore that requires miles of walking on the spot. Up and down their knees go, squashing soapy water through mounds of tangled fabric. The bathtub has distinct zones. Different degrees of dirty water. One area is soap-powder blue whilst another almost black, and beneath the taps it is clearer. The coldness of the water seems to make the cloth heavier and they struggle to heave a bath towel out of the clutches of some pinstriped flared trousers. Slopping it down with a splash, they trudge some more.

To make things more comfortable, although at the risk of being shouted at, they turn on the hot water tap. This makes the immersion heater react loudly as the guzzling tank refills with cold water. So they open the tap fully to get as much heat as they can before their father calls up the stairs ordering them to turn it off. It is a hazardous task too, as large buttons and metal zips often hurt their feet, making them lose balance. The surface of the tub becomes slippery due to the soapy detergent. A misplaced step upon the curved sides of the bath twists ankles. It tends to happen a lot, and always unexpectedly. Carole and Paul create an arch by grasping each other's shoulders, and providing neither of them has got head lice, put their heads together. Initially they did this out of tiredness for extra balance but lately it has become part of a game. Left, right, left, right, left, right they march, steadily getting faster and faster until practically running. Their heads bump together and only when their laughter, or the splashing, becomes too much do they halt, panting like eager puppies. Of all the chores this is Paul's least favourite, although technically he doesn't really have a favourite. In the end the clothes are cleaned, the bath tub gleams and their feet feel velvety smooth. Once the laundry is rinsed, wrung and hung the two are free to play outside.

The street is all but empty of playmates. Paul's brothers are nowhere to be seen and Clive is not at home. Paul gathers some newspaper from under the cushion of his father's armchair to burn in the living-room fireplace. He isn't cold, he's just bored. He tears up bits of cardboard and, leaning sticks of wood against the tiled hearth, stamps down hard to snap them into pieces. He is careful to turn his face with every stomp because the painful memory of a flying plank and a whack to the forehead makes him overly cautious. The flickers are slow to catch on and Paul soon grows weary of watching the ballet-dancing flames struggle to take hold. He covers the mouth of the fireplace with a sheet of newspaper. Starved of oxygen, the fire sucks up a draught through the gaps. The fed flames then bellow aggressively. The newspaper sheet pulls inward. It turns orange and the centre suddenly ignites. Paul lets go, allowing the air current to draw it in and the burning page is carried straight up the chimney. Paul can see quite a way up the stack before the glow is swallowed by the black.

Today, for some reason, these fiery delights are short-lived. Paul's restless nature can find no joy. A melancholic mood washes over him. Suppressed thoughts and frustrations battle for attention. He generally denies them both. As a rule, he refuses to acknowledge any of life's unpleasantness, attempting to banish dissatisfaction by ignoring it, which takes an awful lot of effort, especially on days with little distraction. Paul is expectant that life will change for the better when he grows up. Once he leaves school he'll be free to do whatever he wants. But today is not a day to count the days: there are far too many. His optimism is at a low. On these occasions, when solitude and sorrow collide, graphic images and anxieties mobilise.

Paul recalls the day before his sixth birthday a cute black kitten being thrown out of an upstairs window. It landed with such force on the concrete path, it didn't move. It was later put out of its misery, drowned in a bucket of water next to the back door. There is often harshness in working-class households. Mark took Paul's frog and threw it onto the roof to annoy him. Paul could hear it hopping about in the metal guttering. Then it leaped over the side, splatted on the ground and was savaged by Red. This was also put out of its misery. Paul used a spade and, in one fell swoop, sliced the poor thing in two. He buried it in the garden and made a cross out of two ice-lolly sticks to mark the grave.

Paul decides not to add more fuel to the fire. Instead he chooses to clean out the fireplace. He scrapes up the ashes, pops them in the dustbin outside and continues to sweep away the dust. A while passes before he is alerted by some quick, urgent knocks at the window. Darren is calling for assistance. The bin has caught fire next to the side gate and is burning the fence. They quickly connect the hosepipe and the flames are drenched, the hissing smoke billowing upwards. The melted bin has folded in on itself. Huge lava-like shards, solidified mid-flow to hang listlessly, and plastic splotches mark the surrounding grass and slabs. It is totally unsalvageable. Paul's dad is fuming when he comes home from his pigeon club meeting. The bin was relatively new, not long issued by the council to replace the old metal ones. It also had 'NO HOT ASHES' embossed onto the lid. To Paul's surprise no punishment is forthcoming. His father overlooks his stupidity because he regards Paul's intentions of cleaning the fireplace as good. Paul thinks it best not to mention lighting the fire because he felt bored.

Within hours the crumpled black mass is replaced by a dustbin taken from the rear garden of number sixteen, another vacant property. It takes but two strokes of white paint to revise the bin's ownership, which now reads forty-six. Sort of proving that not everything the children drag home is useless trash. Some things are quite practical and show the children to be thoughtful. Council houses tend to be fitted with the same interiors so cupboard drawers or detachable window panes can easily be unscrewed and swapped with broken ones at home. They replaced their toilet seat when one of the brackets cracked. This is not considered stealing, more requisitioning, therefore their father issues warnings with only a dash of irritation. "Just make sure you don't get caught," is all he has to say on that particular score.

***

"Honk, honk!" Paul uses the not-so-secret goose-call to inform Clive that he is waiting in the street. The resonant sound is able to penetrate exterior walls and still be heard over the squabbling going on inside Clive's house.

They stroll up the road heading nowhere in particular. After struggling to heave open the red door of a public telephone box, they enter. Clive clowns around coughing with his tongue lolling out. Choking, he attempts to waft away the strong stench of urine. Paul shows off a neat trick he's learnt by watching his brothers. He dials the numbers one and six, a service called Dial-a-Disc. He waits for the peeps that indicate he should insert a ten pence piece, but instead of using money he pushes a wooden ice-lolly stick into the slot. By knocking a small spring-loaded knob at the top of the slot, the phone registers payment. It takes a little practice before Clive is also able to connect a call. If it is done too quickly or too slowly it doesn't work. They listen to some music and dial a few random numbers, mimicking whoever picks up the other end. Paul wiggles the lollipop stick up the chute where the returned coins fall out. Nothing happens so he stuffs in an empty crisp packet to block the hole. Maybe next time he passes, removing it may yield some cash.

Unfortunately, Paul's plan to steal phone change from unsuspecting callers doesn't pan out. As favourite pastimes go, waiting isn't one of them. It can't be more than fifteen minutes before he returns. After which they enter a small gap between the thick bushes and a high fence that surrounds the car-park of his dad's local, the Beckley Tavern. Hidden from view they are able to sneak around the back of the building to an outside storage area. Towering above them, crates of empty bottles and spent beer-barrels await collection. Paul snatches a pop bottle and, without being seen, they backtrack out of there. Through a side entrance of the pub, a section called *the outdoor,* they pass the bottle through a small hatch to the barmaid. They receive the ten pence deposit on it which is immediately spent on some chewy Black Jacks and Fruit Salad sweets. Clive reckons Black Jacks are better than Fruit Salads but Paul doesn't agree. They weigh up the merits. Paul tells Clive that Black Jacks taste manky and Fruit Salads yummy. Clive counters with the 'yeah but' fact that Black Jacks make your mouth black. On reflection, Paul capitulates, adding one final fact that Fruit Salads still look nicer. Clive nods and chews, showing off his teeth which are black.

Such debates regarding their theories, latest discoveries and important recreational decisions have become normal between the two. With their siblings they instinctively argue and oppose but with each other they discuss, weigh up options and generally arrive at a mutual agreement. In this manner they decide that another jaunt through the underground tunnels might be a good way to occupy time.

Paul rushes home to fetch the flashlight bulb and battery he hides in his treasure box. Clive, to avoid capture as he's supposed to be grounded, plans to meet him at the entrance to the sewer. Paul runs all the way home, seeing if he can be quick enough to beat Clive to the end of the brook. It's a race day and Paul can hear his dad in the back garden attempting to coax a pigeon down from a rooftop by rattling the tin of bird feed. "C'mon, c'mon, c'mon then." Paul is not meant to go round the back in case he scares the birds, and the frustration in his father's voice today advises him not to push his luck.

He gets held up waiting for Carole to answer the front door. Blocked from using the back garden, the alleyway is off-limits. Nor is it possible for him to sneak through any gardens with so many people out enjoying the sunshine. Paul is forced to go the long way around. Over Windsor Park he meets the kite man who gives him a lift on his pushbike. Paul precariously balances on the front section of the bicycle saddle, his feet gripping the down bar as they roll along the inclined path, making good speed. The man cups Paul's crotch to pull him back onto the seat, telling him he is concerned he'll slip off the saddle and knock his goolies against the gear changer. He does this several times before reaching the bottom of the path. Paul then dismounts, thanks him for the lift and waves goodbye.

Using the glow from the bulb, Clive and Paul are able to see well enough to run through the tall section of the tunnel. Step, step, jump, they curve their way along, avoiding the central flow as they snake beneath the heels and wheels of those above-ground. The slimy ramp is still a little worrisome but, with a good run up and a leap of faith, neither of them slips on the green, wet surface. Assisted by light, the distortions of time and distance are reset and traversing through the tunnel is considerably quicker. They soon exit into the open channel and, as before, have to squat on their haunches to cross underneath the awkwardly low bridge. Coming in the opposite direction and bouncing with each step, they meet Darren and Stephen carrying a rolled-up carpet upon their narrow shoulders.

"Where'd you get that?" Paul is curious to know.

"Mind your own business," Darren is quick to interject before Stephen's reply leaves his mouth. "Don't tell 'em anything," he adds, "they'll only follow."

Darren may have a point.

The elder brothers continue on without breaking their stride. Clive and Paul step aside and watch them go, the heavy carpet sagging in the middle. Without assistance it is a proper struggle for Darren and Stephen to crouch, raise the carpet and walk beneath the low bridge without it touching the water. Hearing Darren and Stephen bicker about lifting the ends up higher makes the young boys snigger.

They proceed onwards. As they are about to enter the next underground section of sewers, they meet Mark and Jason lugging a bulky gas fire. It is a large, wooden-framed fire which somehow they have managed to squeeze through a manhole and carry down the horseshoe steps to transport it thus far. Panting and showing annoyance, Mark orders Paul to help. Clive also grabs a corner. With four the chore is made easy. They carry it under the road bridge without touching the water and even succeed in hauling it up and out of the high-walled concrete channel.

At home the carpet, a brown and orange synthetic monstrosity, waits to be laid on the living room floor. The gas fire is placed on the hearth in front of the open coal fire, and although Bill connects it up to the gas mains without incident, the odd whiff of gas is ever present.

Chapter Twenty: Scrumping

It's turning out to be a bumper summer of sunshine. The back garden is dotted with ladybirds, so many that collecting them in jars is no longer of interest. Clive is wearing his duffle-coat; he and Paul are out on a trek. It became a trek the moment they stumbled across a heap of newly hacked shrubs. Suitable for intrepid explorers of dense jungles and rugged trails, they set about yanking, snapping and twisting the branches until they come away with a couple of staffs. Stripping the bark off their walking sticks gives them both a lot of pleasure as shaving sticks, as most kids know, is a very satisfying thing to do. Clive and Paul possess the exact same penknives, miniature ones with white oyster-shell handles. Paul's blade has a keen edge as he has recently sharpened it. Many times, whilst putting away the cutlery, he's seen the strange contraption with its turning metal discs. A weird item that is neither used as a pokey-stirring thing nor a cutting tool. By watching his father draw a blade across the wheels he finally discovered what it is used for. Although how it actually sharpens knives makes absolutely no sense. Paul tested his knife's edge by scoring it across his thumb, the way he'd seen his dad do it. Blood oozed from the stinging wound. Thankfully, nurse Carole was close at hand to devise a Band Aid plaster using a strip of newspaper held in place by a piece of string.

Heading in the direction of Beckley Park, Clive and Paul stroll, letting a trail of curled, stripped bark fall behind them. Tucked directly behind Beckley Tavern is another ill-equipped play area often devoid of children, mainly a green, uncut field that occupies a gap between the council properties of Paul's area and the private houses of the middle classes. Clive pauses a moment, amused by some white dog poo. He pokes at it with the point of his stick, attempts to skewer the stool, but like a lump of mature cheese it crumbles. Unimpressed, the two continue. Swiping and lashing at the flora, although mainly for effect, they enter a secluded pathway leading off one corner of the park. This overgrown short-cut, a jungle trail of dangling branches suffused with an overbearing aroma of elderflowers, feels relatively chilly in the morning shade. Strewn with litter this green corridor of dilapidated fences, broken gates and nettles has become a bit of a dumping ground. Sawn branches and mounds of cut grass block access to many gardens and keep all but the determined from straying off the path.

On the lookout for apples they scour the skyline. The very first tree they come across is occupied by two scrumpers. Darren and Stephen, in among the branches, are lobbing apples. Heading in their direction issuing clear instructions to bugger off is an old man waving a garden rake. They drop down and scarper. Jumping over the collapsed fence, they then tussle with some brambles. Clive and Paul, having absolutely nothing to do with the incident, happily step aside. Amused, they look on, exchanging glances but no words with the two escapees. Their efforts to display that they just so happen to be passing by are rewarded. The old man pays no attention to the two shabby onlookers.

Back in the street, there are many individuals out enjoying the sizzling sunshine. The adults are mostly occupied with gossiping and the toddlers with toddling. 'Many Rivers To Cross', a tune by Jimmy Cliff, streams across the scene. Mr Abraham is out polishing his pride and joy, a gold-coloured Austin Princess motorcar. The music comes from his house.

With each passing year the ownership of new and used cars increases within Britain, exclusively the latter along Paul's road. Symbols of prosperity adorn the kerb outside many homes. The fathers of Martin Murphy and the twins from the grove both now own a car. Ideal when playing a game of hide and seek or knock and run, but these cherished motors tend to warrant much space and respect. Many of the children, including Paul, have witnessed Mr Abraham raging when the ball accidentally hits his car. In Paul's opinion he is a horrible man with a fierce, intimidating scowl. A man whose violent relationships often spill out into the street. So when the children play gutters they tend to avoid his house and congregate nearer the bottom of the cul-de-sac.

Today there's a gathering of well over a dozen. In amongst them are Ginger Charley, Crybaby Kenny and his sister, Mandy. Martin and Debbie Murphy are also there, along with a cousin named Keith. Twins Glen and Pamela, munching something Paul guesses to be sugary, are chatting with Carole who seems to have made a couple of new friends, James and Belinda. They come from a children's home situated on the main road. Paul is surprised to learn there is an orphanage so close by, one that backs onto the alleyway at the bottom of his garden. Also from the main road, with strict instructions not to play in the back streets, is a skinny girl called Becky Harris and her friend, the girl with frizzy hair, Wanda Davies. Paul had seen her once before through his bedroom window back when forty-six was still an empty house. Both girls appear to be around Paul's age though show no interest in Clive and Paul. They seem more concerned in making the right sort of eyes at Darren and Stephen, who are busy peeling the skin off a cooking apple using their top front teeth. Also within the chattering mix are Mark and Jason. In one manner or another this nifty pack of elite raiders, the newly formed Scrumpers' Union, decides it should carry out an expedition. One to locate fruit wherever it may hang: in other words, scrumping en masse. As the mob heads out the levels of bravado and nervous excitement rise. Surprisingly, the whole group, led by Charley, still manage to sneak below his kitchen window, through the garden and over the back wall without hearing any yelling or furious window thumping.

In the back park, they wade through knee-high grass towards the apples they've seen hanging beyond the wiry barbs and cemented glass shards — perimeter fence adornments to stop trespassers entering private gardens. The girls, deemed the fairer sex and therefore unsuited to clamber over fences or, if required, run at speed, are look-outs. Clive's duffle coat is placed over the barbed wire as a barrier between the sharp metal and the children's skin. This allows the bigger kids, with a bunk up, to clamber into the garden with relative ease. A torrent of apples follows, flying over the fence and dropping like hail stones, occasionally striking the collectors scampering about to recover them. In less than one minute the raiders are back in the park, hyped-up and laughing. When retrieved, Clive's duffle coat snags on the wire leaving a finger-sized hole in the hood. Unconcerned or maybe just happy to have it back, he instantly dons his protective cover despite the blistering heat.

In an attempt to prove himself, Ginger Charley, who is often a bit of a numbskull, announces he can easily scale the corner fence to obtain some pears. Perhaps past events play a part in the cheers that egg him on, yet true to his boast with two quick steps and a jump he scurries like a mouse up a curtain over and into the garden. In a flash he bounds straight back into the park slapping his head, crotch, legs and back as if on fire. In his frenzied attempt to beat off a swarm of bees, he approaches the group who scatter with yelps of terrified hysterics. There is no assistance or sympathy forthcoming from the disbanding Scrumpers' Union. Screams of "Don't come near!" are all that he hears. Charley, out of pain, not shame, turns an even deeper scarlet than usual and is left to hobble off home all alone in a flood of tears.

Advancing towards Windsor's playing fields, the panting children regroup and someone suggests a visit to the Woodlands. The entrance to this mini forest lies a little beyond the sewerage tunnel at the furthest edge of Windsor Park. So firstly the children scout around the outer boundary of the park, checking for unlocked gates and hedgerow holes. Discretion, not being any kind of a point, neither weak nor strong, has them trampling along in a huge group, necks craned to search the skyline for fruit trees, calling out and jumping up to look into people's gardens.

They raid a blackberry bramble of its fruit. *Nom, nom, nom,* noises akin to a trough load of greedy piglets temporarily silence any real chatter. Hand scratches and crimson fingers are a small price to pay for the juicy berries.

"Er narrrsty." Carole points out the white splats of bird poo on some of the leaves.

"Errr, there's some 'ere too," Becky Harris shrieks, indicating more to where Paul has just been eating than the actual poo.

"Urgh, you've got yacky germs," Wanda squeals, and Paul watches as those nearest shout "Jabs," whilst feigning a medical injection to the upper-arm. This well-known safeguard is often utilised to stave off the dreaded lurgey, an unspecified, highly contagious disease that Paul must now surely possess. He quickly leaps to rid himself of the contaminant by touching Clive's sleeve. Now free he also adds the same protection by striking his own shoulder and calling out "Jabs." An impromptu game of chase instantly erupts. Screeches, screams and protests, which last for around twenty metres or so, until Jason shouts out, "APPLES!" Then the whole group adopts a serious, stealth-like manner. Beyond some bushes and a low rickety gate await four trees. An abundance of cooking apples dangle close to the ground near the gate. Further in is a second tree of rosy red apples, another of green, and also a pear tree, with no sign of bees. The bravest, big kids, to which group Clive and Paul strongly believe they belong, head straight up the garden path towards the pear tree that has been planted nearer to the house. The rest wait in the park, daring every so often to dart inside to snatch a low-hanging cooking apple. Colliding into one another their fits of laughter threaten to give the game away. Nobody has brought along a bag so once again Clive's duffle coat comes in handy. He opens it out to create a makeshift basket. Together with Paul, they gather up the pears being thrown to the ground by Darren, who is standing upon Mark's shoulders. Jason and Stephen attempt to do the same beneath the red apple tree. They fail when Jason winces and drops his shoulder, sending Stephen crashing to the floor. Stephen howls, moaning about landing on a scabby apple that has given him an excruciating dead-leg. Somewhat perturbed by Jason's laughter, he hobbles out of the garden rubbing his thigh. A rotary mower spluttering to life on a neighbouring lawn unsettles the raiders who beat a hasty retreat. Anxiety about being recognised sees many of the children heading towards home. As the seventies dictate, should news reach their parents that they've been seen trespassing and stealing with the roughnecks from forty-six, they'll surely get a proper lamping.

The Scrumpers' Union disbands and, with unnoticed eye prompts, Mark, Jason, Darren and Stephen suddenly dart off in the direction of the Woodlands. Impeded by their pouch of apples and pears, Clive and Paul are left flat-footed, along with Carole, wispy haired Wanda and skinny Becky. Clive releases a corner of the coat to grab an apple and the other fruit rolls to the ground. He lobs the apple at the fleeing brothers, then Paul joins in and so does Carole. Frustratingly they miss them by miles. With the bulk of the fruit retrieved and stashed in the nose cone of the playground rocket, they decide to pursue the vanished runaways. They sprint out of the park and along the leafy alleyway that leads to the woods. Clive slows, clutching at his ribs and moaning about a side stitch. Paul feels the same pain so they stop running to catch a much needed breath. The girls, who appear immune, complain that the other four are getting away.

They enter the Woodlands, which is basically an open meadow surrounded by small clusters of trees, fully enclosed within a residential zone. An area of large, detached homes with extremely long gardens. It takes no more than twenty minutes to walk the entire circumference of these woodlands. So it doesn't take long before the snapping of a brittle branch alerts Paul and his crew to the whereabouts of their targets. The five squeeze behind a tree, one hardly wide enough to conceal a grown man. With exaggerated shushes for silence they snigger and spy around the trunk. In the lull, which is momentary, Paul lets out a sudden rumble: a fart that, on a breezeless day, would surely have been detected by all in the general vicinity of the woods.

"Taxed!" he proclaims, before anyone has a chance to utter "Tenners." Verbally taxing his flatulence ensures that Paul doesn't receive ten swift punches, which often follow forgetful children who burp and break wind.

"Errr, it smells like crab apples," whispers Wanda.

"Eww, crabby arse that stinks," Becky teases, before slinking away to seek refuge behind a different tree.

The other three quickly follow, and indignantly Paul responds, "Well, the one who smelt it dealt it."

"The one who denied it supplied it," comes Carole's hushed retort.

"Yeah, but whoever spoke last set off the blast," Clive adds.

"Aha, that's you then cause you just... erm..." Paul's words trail off when he realises he should have kept schtum.

All tomfoolery is put aside and vigilance returns when they see the four brothers moving on. In pursuit, as silently as the trampled twigs allow, the snoopers flit from tree to tree. Whenever the brothers enter a garden, Clive, Paul and the girls move in close and peer through gaps in the greenery to observe them. When the lads start to withdraw the spies scatter for the nearest cover. Like it does with so many young children, this type of sneakiness tastes quite delicious to Paul and his friends. The thrill of it rates rather highly in his uneventful life, so the shadowing game continues for a good half hour.

Then Mark spots the distinctive gait of the local bobby entering the top end of the woods. In a panic, he shouts, "PC Spoon! Leg it!" and the brothers rush past the five hidden spies as they sprint away. PC Spoon lives close by. He knows Paul's dad by name. His daughter attends Jason's class at school so if he sees any of the brothers he'll surely recognise them. Perhaps he's been tipped off or maybe he is simply taking a short-cut from the shops on the main road. His steady pace doesn't change so it isn't clear if they've been seen. No one waits to find out. Avoiding the pathways and open ground, they weave through the trees like deer evading a huntsman, only daring to cross grassy glades when concealed by a bend in the footpath. They make it to the dark leafy alleyway without being seen. The girls continue running, but Clive and Paul hold back to check on the progress of PC Spoon. They begin to relax, thinking he's stopped, until he rounds a crook in the path. Trampling on at speed, not daring to look back, they re-enter the playing fields. The girls and their brothers are nowhere in sight. Clive and Paul decide to hide out in the darkened mouth of the sewerage tunnel. It takes a while for their nervous laughter to give way to giggling relief and a little more time is spent trying to decide who will brave the scene to check the coast is clean.

Clack! Splat! Pyang! Someone is throwing rocks. One stone hits the iron bars and metallic echoes resound. Another bounces into the tunnel. Down in a gully, trapped within the entrance, they have no idea where the flingers are. There is no ammunition close at hand. Clive arms himself with the rock at his feet. Paul scours the ground. The nearest stones are outside and several metres away. Another round is fired, giving Paul the stone he seeks. They manage to ascertain the direction of attack. Two boys of similar age to themselves are hiding behind trees that line the bank. Paul isn't a particularly brave child but his young friend Clive is. He suggests they wait for the next assault then rush them before they can reload. Before Paul can answer, the other boys launch a third volley. Clive hardly waits for the stones to settle; he charges out, and Paul follows. They splash along the stream lobbing as they run and bending to pick up more stones and hurling them towards the two boys. Now it is they who are pinned down. How quick the tables turn. Clive and Paul are on the boys like rabid wolves. Paul grabs one boy by his t-shirt and punches him in the face. He backs off, holding his nose. In fear, the other boy tries to deny it was them. Clive shoves him down the bank, making him stumble in the water onto his knees.

"Do you want some more, do ya?" Paul asks, feeling much braver after the fact. The boys are terrified, both are snivelling and as it's a general rule that sobbing signifies surrender, Clive and Paul, magnanimous in victory, allow them to limp off home.

After the scuffle they retrieve the fruit stashed in the playground rocket and head back to the street. They are greeted like conquering heroes although nobody is that fussed about the bounty they'd carried all the way home. The others listen intently about all the danger and action of being chased by PC

Spoon and battling the stone throwers. Paul discovers that scrumping isn't really about pinching apples and pears, it's more about the thrill. Hackles and hairs, and the rising of them. However, the fruit is put to good use. Paul's father instructs Mark to make an apple crumble to be eaten at Sunday teatime. He wraps the unripened pears in newspaper and places them in a box in the airing cupboard. In one week the rock-hard pears are soft, sticky and deliciously juicy.

Chapter Twenty-One: Slugs and Snails

Paul is now in Class Five. It is already spring. Autumn and winter have passed by in the usual way. A bonfire in November followed by Christmas, a mildly disappointing one because Paul still didn't receive the Etch-A-Sketch he longs for. Then came a severe January, where snowdrifts reached record highs and cold snaps reached record lows. Fortunately there was only one incident of burst water pipes. The children had to fill the kettle with fresh, untrodden snow from the bottom of the garden to make tea and the circular stain on the kitchen ceiling grew a touch wider. After which Paul's dad came by a paraffin heater, which he lit during the freezing nights thus avoiding any further ruptures.

Paul no longer cares to travel to school with Carole, instead he prefers to call for his classmate, Shane. When Paul knocks at weekends, Shane's parents always say he's not allowed out. Occasionally he's permitted to play on the pavement directly outside his house but strictly forbidden to wander any further. Paul has accepted that his friend will never venture to the bottom of the cul-de-sac and will only ever be a school buddy. Surprisingly, under the guise of working on a class assignment and on the basis that he behaves himself, Shane's parents have relented to his request that they walk to school together.

Their new teacher, Ms Lammers, who possesses a refreshingly calm and flowery disposition, has permitted the class to choose their own projects. Some of the boys have opted to construct a cardboard model of Wembley Football Stadium. Others, mostly girls, have decided to design jewelled crowns, orbs and sceptres to commemorate the Queen's forthcoming jubilee. Since they are free to choose any theme, Paul, pushing the boundaries, gets struck with a sudden flash of inspiration. He proudly takes full credit for his ingenious idea of creating a miniature wildlife sanctuary. That very morning he's salvaged a plastic display case from the back of the shops near the school. He snuck through the teacher's car park, which is strictly out-of-bounds, and concealed it behind the bins with the intention of collecting it at home-time. Laid face down, this see-through cabinet, which is around the size of a sofa cushion, opens and closes like a school desk making it perfect to access his growing colony of slugs and snails. Shane, Paul, and not forgetting Bobby, all strive to devise what they consider to be the perfect habitat. In the bottom they sculpt a generous amount of soil into hills and valleys. Within a small mountain of building rubble they create caves and tunnels, and make bridges from twigs. Over the soil they add a smattering of rotting leaves so their guests can relax out of sight. They even make a small pool from an upturned jam-jar lid should any of them fancy a dip. At the end of day one they have succeeded in establishing a five-star mollusc resort, with four guests: three snails and one slug. However, these numbers steadily grow.

Dawdling to school, hunter-gatherers Shane and Paul forage about the damp patches beneath hedgerows and scour wall crevices seeking out slugs and snails to include in the burgeoning colony. They're spoilt for choice until Paul instructs that only fancy snails or super giant slugs are to be included in the empty margarine tub he holds. Shane struggles to dislodge a determined slug from the bottom of a metal drinks can.

"Naw, that one's rubbish," Paul pipes up.

"But it's really long," argues Shane.

"Yeah, but it's too skinny." Paul is quick to assert his power after reminding Shane exactly whose idea the colony was in the first place. Megalomaniac tendencies mean that he supervises all selections, the act of making the decisions much more important than correctness, or even consistency for that matter. They will only take those he deems worthy. Three pavement-stranded worms make the cut, as do a selection of woodlice, or at least the ones they are quick enough to capture after lifting up a tile of tree bark. A centipede wriggles off unimpeded. Paul has heard somewhere that they can burn you with acid venom. With their new wildlife, strip of tree bark, more decaying leaves and other rotting things, such as a tooth-scored apple core, they arrive at school moments before the bell.

Almost ritually, each time Paul lifts the lid of his insect home to add more residents a crowd of students gather. Repulsed by the slimy trails and mildew stench they point and gag. When a squirming snail is pushed under their noses, the girls shriek and squeal. It seems as if they enjoy being chased around the classroom because, unlike kiss chase, they run a lot slower and with a little less dread. Paul's wayward behaviour earns him a small amount of kudos amongst the boys, and as there really isn't a great deal of it in his life, he often seeks to maintain it with similar pranks and general silliness. As class projects go, the Social Scroungers' snail garden is surely the most intoxicating.

***

Another interesting project Class Five are involved in is cheese making. Ms Lammers has decided to use the surplus milk left over from the class quota to make cottage cheese. Collected in a crate, these spare bottles are stowed in the store room until required. Paul isn't too happy about this as it means missing out on a second bottle. He usually looks forward to the school caretaker arriving to collect the empties. Mr Moody often bestows the gift of an extra bottle, providing the children can gulp it down quick enough.

Ms Lammers and the students are away on a day trip. As payment was required Bobby and Paul have been left behind. Normally they would be inserted into another class and made to sit at the back, but not today. Today they have been given some mathematical worksheets and, for the most part, left in their own classroom, unsupervised. Resentful and annoyed at having to study whilst everyone else is having fun, they vindictively play out a rebellious deed. The morning milk delivered by caretaker Mr Moody falls prey to their ingenious plot. Exchanging fresh for sour, they place the curdling bottles in the middle of the crate. Upon the class's return, they issue a whispered warning to a select number of friends, informing them to only choose bottles that sit on the outer edges of the crate.

It doesn't take long before complaints about funny-tasting milk ring out. At first, much to the delight of those in the know, these claims are met with, "Don't be so silly, just drink it!" As the obedient twist in their seats attempting to suck putrid liquid through straws, simmering chuckles and hushed voices bubble. Eventually, due to the unsettled fidgeting and growing number of protests, Ms Lammers has no alternative but to pay heed to the grumblers. The class are instructed to put down their drinks. Protests of "Mine tastes fine," echo around the room as Sarah Goody Two-shoes is sent to fetch the caretaker. Bobby and Paul exchange worried glances. Mr Moody informs Ms Lammers that the foil lids are embossed with a letter to indicate the batch. He says that there has been a mix up as not all of them are the same. The culprits feel they are surely done for, yet somehow they manage to evade capture.

Outside the smell of mown lawns fills the air. Nothing says summer is on its way more than the scent of cut grass drying in the sunshine. The cuttings become a precious commodity amongst the children. Panic-gathering, the girls flap about like birds collating heaps of it. Pulling it about themselves they sit brooding in ostrich-size nests. The boys think nest-making is dull and that grass fights are much more fun. They arm themselves with clumps that are still soggy, knowing from experience that they hold together better as they are flung towards their intended targets. Some of the allergic kids rush from the battlefield and head over to the tarmac to avoid the irritating particles being blown around. Desperately attempting to fend off the marauding pillagers, the girls scream complaints as the boys grab handfuls of their neatly gathered cuttings. Realising the futility, the girls join in to fight a battle they have half a chance of winning and the field becomes a hazy war zone of red flashing pullovers and green debris.

Paul may be friendly towards worms but wasps are not so lucky. After annihilating the girl's nests and chasing away foes in a grass battle, the Social Scroungers decide to eliminate what they consider to be vicious pests. Stalking winged creatures they dash about stamping on unsuspecting victims the moment they touch down on a bloom. Sadly the boys haven't learned that bumbles are not the only bee and therefore slaughter with impunity many innocent insects. Hidden from view down in the grass ditch, they cremate the recently squished on miniature funeral pyres.

Paul's penchant for flames means the outline of a box of matches can often be perceived sticking through his trousers. The distinctive rattle is quelled by a scrunched up piece of paper to ensure teachers remain unaware. Pocketed for a hundred and one burning desires, although smoking is not one of them. Paul hasn't yet progressed to sparking up cigarette stubs he finds in the gutter. Scorched fingers and accidental burns are terribly painful but this does not deter Paul's fixation with dancing embers. Disregarding the obvious pleasures, such as incineration and producing bellows of black smoke, Paul obtains much joy from a cheap box of matches. Striking a match and quickly throwing it hard to a concrete floor before it is fully lit produces a sharp, snapping sound much like a firecracker. Taking his penknife Paul can whittle off flakes of the matchstick's head to be inserted into a cap-gun in place of caps. Better still, as he's discovered by watching his brothers, he can make a hand grenade with two metal bolts and a nut. Twisting the nut a couple of turns onto the top of a bolt creates a small chamber. Broken match-heads are inserted and the second bolt screwed on just tight enough so it doesn't rattle. This produces a missile that, when thrown against a hard surface, explodes with volume. When dashed against the walls of a walkway between two houses the explosion is ear-splitting. Alternatively, simply bashing match-heads with a round rock makes a pretty loud bang and also produces a satisfying spark.

Stimulating other senses, Paul enjoys the burning tingle and salty sulphur hit he receives each time his tongue makes contact with the sandpapery edge that runs along the box's spine. Often he licks it to excess until it's tasteless. With regard to safety-matches, the name alone saps fun, and as he's unable to strike them on any surface, they hold no interest. Although, with persistence and technique Paul knows they can be ignited using the smooth surface of a window pane.

Upon hearing the end of play whistle, they stamp out the smouldering corpses and frantically kick away any evidence before rushing to line up with the other children. They watch the pupils from Class Seven trotting back and forth carrying tables. Festivities for the queen's silver jubilee are being organised up and down the country in the form of garden parties. Paul's school is also celebrating, with a huge outdoor event in the junior's playground. Much like the Christmas party, there are rows of decorated trestle tables. Union jack flags pinned to their edges flutter in the breeze. Overhead red, white and blue bunting flaps rapidly whenever the wind picks up. Jewelled orbs and sceptres, artwork created by the girls, adorn the classroom windows. Numerous portraits of Her Majesty smile out upon the scene of the girls wearing their silver crowns. Their excitement is palpable.

At the back of the queue sword-fighting chair legs clatter and clash. The children of Class Five are eager to march with their seats in an orderly fashion across the playground to the waiting feast. The infants from Yellow, Blue and Green Classes enter the playground led by their teachers. A military parade of well-behaved toddlers position themselves around one of the smaller, lower tables. When it finally comes time for Class Five to join the party, two of them are excluded. The cheesy milk saga, smoke billowing from down the ditch or destroying the girl's grass nests may have been to blame, but the reason given is simply that naughty children don't deserve treats. Sulking faces etched with regret watch the party-goers enjoying the cakes. Eventually Ms Lammers' heart thaws, she relents and allows Bobby and Paul to join their classmates.

The following Saturday, out in the street, the tenants' association organise their jubilee party. A members-only event, or so it seems, as Paul's family haven't been invited. Paul watches the commotion with a tinge of jealousy and a sense of betrayal. Clive is there stuffing his face. His family were invited, but despite the goodies on offer he soon gets bored sitting still around the table. He pops back and forth intermittently for a quick chat with Paul, but each time neglecting to smuggle him any of the iced cupcakes. Cakes that Paul adamantly assures himself he doesn't want anyway. At least Paul has seen Queen Elizabeth, albeit a vague memory. A picnic, in a park along with Carole and his father. Running up and rolling down a sloped grass verge near a busy road and, of course, Her Majesty the Queen dressed in green. It must have been a long time ago when he lived at twenty-two as his recall shows but three hazy images. Still, the fact satisfies him knowing that none of his friends can claim the same.

Chapter Twenty-Two: Shopping

Today is a day of mixed fortunes. St Jude's Church is holding a jumble sale but unfortunately for Carole and Paul there is an entrance fee: two pence for children and five for adults. Luckily Mrs McGaveridge lives right next door but she's out. Carole and Paul have already called round four times in the hopes of her return. As noon approaches they try one last time then give up. The church sale is almost over, the hall empty but for a few nattering women sitting behind tables of bric-à-brac and drinking tea. On seeing the two milling around the entrance they waive the door charge to allow Carole and Paul free range to rummage through the cast-offs and unsold objects. On a central table a tangled mass of jumble, piled high and reaching low, has been left to rest where it fell. The bulk of it appears mostly suitable for old women and babies. The stale smell of the dusty fabrics deters them from turning over any more than the first few items. Paul holds open a large floral granny dress, and with enthusiastic nodding and a devious grin he suggests that it would suit Carole. She pulls out an equally hideous blouse and holds it up against Paul's body as if to measure the two. He swipes it from her, dashing it back onto the pile before moving on. There are a lot of ladies' shoes, sandals and stiletto heels left over but nothing suitable for Carole. Momentarily considering their father they sift through them looking for a pair of men's shoes for him. It matters not that they don't know his correct size because all they find is a single, brown, dried-out leather one with a curled up sole. They giggle at the notion of a one-legged man hopping around shoeless. Paul tells Carole to smell it. She declines. Amongst the odds and sods are some broken toys and cracked ornaments. They find nothing worth buying, which suits their budget of zero pence. Spending only time, they leave empty-handed.

Although it is a lovely sunny day, the street is empty of suitable playmates and Clive isn't at home. In the back garden, Darren and Paul's father are busy in the pigeon pen scraping out the roosts and nesting boxes, clearing them of bird droppings. Sweeping up piles of dried excrement often throws up dust and microscopic mites, making the air in the pen taste foul. Today Paul feels very fortunate not to be his dad's pet. As they clean the racing pigeons are flying back from Thurso in Scotland, due to arrive sometime tomorrow. To encourage them to fly faster, his dad has used nesting hens, eager to return to their eggs. While they're away, the eggs of unfortunate surrogates, deemed inferior, are taken away and replaced with those of the champion birds. Then, shortly before the mothers return, the eggs are reinstated in the nesting box and the birds are none the wiser, or so it would seem.

As the two eldest brothers are nowhere to be seen and Darren is busy with his father, Carole and Paul are sent to Mac Market to purchase groceries. Due to financial constraints the items the family purchases are never premium products. Left on the shelf, chocolate biscuits, yogurts and top brand cereal are for the trolleys of what the children consider posh people. Instead, they buy uninspiring cheap products, mainly tinned.

The supermarket wasn't always there. Paul can clearly recall a rainy day incident when he and Darren were clambering over the mounds of rubble belonging to the picture-house that once occupied the space. Paul was around five at the time and had accompanied Darren to fetch a sack of pigeon corn from the pet shop near Paul's school. Actually, to be precise it was a brown paper bag not a sack. One that became rain-soaked and decided to split as they clambered over the wall that enclosed the demolition site. The grains began to scatter everywhere and, due to the site being positioned on the brow of a hill, much of the pigeon corn rolled down it. A dreaded urgency washed over them. Darren attempted to keep the splitting bag intact whilst instructing Paul to scrape together as much corn as he could before it all got swept along the gutter to the drain. In the pelting rain Paul hastily scooped up handfuls of the feed. One small mercy was that the flatter pieces of yellow maize didn't really roll. Darren then sent Paul running around the corner to ask the greengrocer for another bag. He swiftly returned with a second brown paper bag which also became wet, threatening to rip once again. Paul's father was livid when he heard their explanations. He'd actually warned the three eldest to keep off the building site, saying it was too dangerous. Paul escaped punishment that time but Darren did not.

In further reminiscence of the old picture-house, Paul recalls attending The Saturday Morning Picture Show. It was on his fifth birthday. He went on the stage with the other birthday children and received a lucky-bag containing sweets and small toys. It was a proper treat because in Paul's house they don't really celebrate birthdays. They do, however, always receive a birthday card. Their father places the envelope by the front door as if it has been delivered by the postman, addressed to the relevant child with the street name and door number written on it. A nice idea, however the ruse no longer fools any of the family, due to the absence of a postage stamp.

Carrying the bog-standard shopping list, Carole and Paul wheel their trolley into the store. All echoes of the old picture-house blown away in the dust from the demolition have been replaced with the hum of fluorescent lighting and metallic clanks of supermarket bustle. They proceed to place the following items into the cart: a hefty ten-pound sack of potatoes, weight not price, and two Fray Bentos steak and kidney pies which come in a tin. These are soon joined by two large cans of garden peas and another of baby carrots, ingredients for their Sunday dinner. Then, prompted by memories of bread strikes and bare shelves displaying nothing but a few loaves of yucky brown, quick-thinking Carole urges Paul to rush off to fetch two jumbo loaves of white. Nobody in Paul's family likes brown bread and he can well remember the delicious smell that lingered when his dad attempted to remedy this by baking his own bread. A mouthwatering memory of a delectable feast, fresh warm loaves not long out of the oven.

By the time he returns Carole has added four family-sized cans of baked beans. Paul balances the loaves on top so they don't get crushed. At the dairy section they acquire one dozen eggs, a giant tub of margarine and a packet of Dad's special not-to-be-touched butter. Next they add two packets of granulated white sugar and three packets of PG Tips tea, always loose leaf and never teabags. Their father can't abide teabags; he always says, "It just isn't proper." Then they add eight cans of evaporated milk to the trolley. With a glare of revulsion Paul adds a sack of Wheat-a-Flakes and Carole, two jars of jam, one mixed fruit the other strawberry. On the way to the cold meat and cheese counter, they pick up a bottle of low calorie orange squash. Carole takes a ticket and waits for her number to come up. She is to buy half a pound of sliced luncheon meat and a pound of mild cheddar cheese. Paul wanders off. He lurks behind towers of produce whilst Carole wheels around the store wondering where he is. He skids up and down the neighbouring aisles, playing hide and seek. When the shop is empty, like today, he often bowls the heavy metal cans of dog-food across the floor towards her. He gleans much satisfaction skilfully rolling them without them spinning out and crashing into the sides of the lanes. Carole gets a little flustered when Paul bowls six large cans in quick succession, each one accurately aimed at her feet.

Paul normally envies the *posh* families whose trolleys are lavished with luxury items. However, today their father must have been feeling generous, or perhaps flush. After a heartfelt plea he has permitted the children to purchase four packets of Smiths salt-and-vinegar flavoured chip-sticks. A special lunchtime treat served with fried eggs and tinned peas.

At the checkout the children place the groceries onto a small counter. The cashier lifts each item to view the price sticker, clunks the buttons on the till and then places the object into a second trolley. Hanging from it, Paul notices a handbag, which has obviously been left by the previous customer. Obscured from sight by the mini table, the cashier hasn't seen it and neither has Carole. Paul imagines the bag holds a purse containing lots of money. As Carole is busy paying, he pushes the trolley a little way out of sight and shoves the handbag inside, concealing it beneath the two jumbo loaves. His action requires no justification; he soothes his conscience with the rhyme *Finders keepers, losers weepers.* He is sure Carole will want to do the right thing and tell the cashier about it so waits until they are out of the supermarket before informing her.

They use the zebra crossing to cross the busy road, turning the trolley backwards and lifting the rear wheels to pull it on to the ramp of the slanted kerb. Along the steep inclined footpath, Paul pushes and Carole pulls. They roll past the low wall and hedges that lead up to the garages and continue through the estate towards the mouth of the alley that leads to their house. They've made this trip countless times. The local residents are used to hearing the rackety noise made by the weekly shopping as it bumps along the uneven paving slabs. Houses either side of the alleyway must also be familiar with the loud clashing from when they descend the four steps. Removing the eggs, they give the trolley a slight push and allow gravity to do the rest. The first step is a single one and, providing the weight distribution favours the rear of the kart, the trolley rolls and bumps down without tipping over. The same goes for the second step. However, the last two follow in quick succession. It requires a light touch to reduce the speed, and as a safety measure, Paul's hand hovers above the handle should it by chance decide to tip forward.

The anticipation of what goodies the handbag contains has to simmer a while longer. Paul hasn't dared to look, fearful that someone might see. He rushes to hide the bag amongst the rubbish littering the dead-end of the alley. Parked up alongside a second, empty trolley at the bottom gate, the children begin loading up their arms with produce. Paul bounds along the path to the house; back and forth he goes, completing the errand with much enthusiasm. Once the shopping has been stowed away their dad, irked that they hadn't bothered to return the other trolley to the store, orders them to do so. Now Paul can return to his booty. Excitement bursting from him he retrieves the bag. Visualising wads of cash he eagerly pulls on the zip. A flash of disappointment follows. There is no purse and no cash. The handbag contains only a used carrier-bag and an empty one at that. His hopes dashed he does the same, slamming the handbag onto the pile of trash.

Carole and Paul clatter back up the alleyway, their empty trolleys rattling much more noisily than loaded ones. Carole, a few steps behind, pushes hers quite normally whilst Paul, venting his frustration, gives mighty thrusts before letting go of the handle. His kart lunges as far forward as his power permits before rolling backwards to meet his catch. Sometimes a wheel decides to judder, making the trolley veer off into the fence. Bashing and banging, this clamorous action is repeated as they amble along the incline, only stopping when Paul reaches the steps. Out in the open they run along the pavement to gather more speed. The race is on. Leaning over the handle, a counterbalance to prevent doing wheelies and falling on their backsides, they park their feet on the under tray beside the rear wheels and glide through the estate. The trolley turning sideways and hitting the kerb is to be avoided at all costs. Paul has learnt that painful lesson twice already. Now scooting through the garages, Carole, ever optimistic, heads towards the corner for another quick check for abandoned babies. After rolling past the hedges and low wall, down the incline and over the zebra crossing they reach Mac Market, or at least the outer edges of the plot, and with one almighty push from each of them they return the two trolleys. Paul's delivery is straight and direct, his trolley coming to a stop not too far from the front door. Carole's is angled and wandering. It rolls into the car park — a rather steep-sloping car park. They hear no immediate screams or shouts, and no crashing sounds ring out, but just to be sure the two rush back over the zebra crossing distancing themselves from what may or may not transpire.

Waving to them from a ground-floor window an old lady beckons them over. She gives them a grocery list, a five pound note and sends the obliging children off to fetch a few provisions. A chance to earn a small gratuity encourages them to be swift, which they are. She gives them two pence each. Carole and Paul both agree the old lady is really, really stingy and that next time she calls, they'll pretend not to hear. With their money Carole buys a multi-coloured sweet necklace which she nibbles on like a rabbit. Paul spends his on a juice-inducing Anglo bubbly and a rock-hard gobstopper. The latter almost cracks his teeth when he fails to prove to Carole he has the strength to bite right through it.

On their return home, there are questions as to where the sweets came from.

"We got them from Stars." Carole's literal response infuriates their displeased father.

"Self, self, self is all you bloody think of." Their father shows his annoyance with the utterance of his one and only swear word. The two remain baffled as to what they have done wrong. Paul offers up an explanation.

"A old lady give us da money, cause we went to the shops for her."

"And you didn't stop to consider the poor dog and pigeons?" Finally it dawns on them that they could have popped into the butcher's and greengrocer's to request some bones and cabbage leaves.

"Oh, we can go now," Carole declares.

Frustrated their father cuts off his own nose.

"Don't bother, they can just go without."

The children know better than to insist and, looking dejected, walk away, secretly happy they don't have to traipse down to the shops for a third time.

Chapter Twenty-Three: Five Pounds

Nothing ever happens. Well, not good stuff anyway. Once again Paul is bored and a little downcast. Even the glorious sunshine is failing to brighten his mood. He's sitting on the front wall swinging his legs and despondently allowing his heels to thump and bounce against its rough surface. He's suffering from envy, as he quite often does. Half watching ten-year-old Jessica Wright and Mandy Cropper playing with a strange contraption. Standing in the road approximately four metres apart, each grasping two handles, the girls take turns opening and closing their arms. When Jessica's arms open, Mandy's close and vice-versa. They do this aerobics display in sync, repeating the motion over and over. These movements produce a rather pleasing whooshing noise as they send a large orange, oval ball made of plastic zipping along two cords. Back and forth it glides, capturing the attention of the children as they begin to emerge from their houses. Paul has been waiting for someone to play with, but instead all the kids mill around Jessica, whose popularity increases with each approved request to have a go.

Paul wishes he had — had better toys, had pocket money, had used a proper stamp to send his entry in for that competition to win *a trip of a lifetime* to Disney World in America. He'd used a secondhand stamp that hardly stuck to the envelope. Every morning for goodness knows how long his hopes are dashed when the postman neglects to deliver his winning confirmation.

Like the other spectators, he too wishes to have a go on the thingamajig, but a sense of family loyalty will not allow him to cavort with the daughter of a sworn enemy. Instead he continues to look on until his jealousy reaches an intolerable level. A level that sends him to seek solace with the only one who cares to listen, Red the dog. Chained up outside the back door, Red can't go anywhere. Paul's captive audience is so attentive. He moans to Red about wishing and always waiting. How he longs for the day he is old enough to leave school. Then he will be free to do and buy whatever he wants. His plans go no further because Paul knows it will be donkey's years before he reaches sixteen. Grateful for the company, ever faithful Red doesn't mind listening. He nudges Paul with his muzzle to let him know he feels his sadness and understands, to a doggy-degree, Paul's frustrations. Self-pity slowly fades. Contemplating Paul's eyes rest on the dog poo caked within the links of Red's chain. This mobilises him into hosing down the slabs and cleaning up the area, which really isn't all the big. Paul doesn't envy Red the dog.

He's never jealous of his sister Carole either. She is presently away being instructed in the ways of women and taught about girlie things and lady days. Their father has decided it would be prudent to enlist the help of a female, after his cack-handed attempt to explain, as he tried to put it, why women are so pale. Therefore, of late Carole has begun visiting Mrs Green, the wife of a fellow pigeon-fancier. In place of a mother she has become a surrogate to enlighten Carole in the subjects their father simply isn't suited to teach. Thus far Carole has spent all of her time ironing, cleaning and babysitting for Mrs Green's youngest child.

From his top step Paul can see James sitting on the back fence of the children's home. James has buck teeth which are larger than Carole's. He also has a newspaper delivery round and is Carole's secret sweetheart. It remains a secret because if one of the three eldest see her alone with a boy, they bossily command her to return home. "Home now!" is all they say, and Carole must always obey because these orders come from their dad.

Paul has been privy to their clandestine romance for a while now. James once invited Carole to tea at the children's home. Unused to invites, she was nervous so Paul went along too, for moral support and to assist with the consumption of any cake. The children aren't often permitted to cross the thresholds of friends but the orphanage staff and other kids were extremely welcoming. Once inside all nerves quickly vanished. Whilst preparations for afternoon tea got underway, they happily ran about the orphanage feeling quite at home. The building constitutes two semi-detached properties that have been knocked through to create one large home, which is excellent for playing hide and seek in. That was when Paul discovered Carole and James kissing behind a door. He paid no heed to their smooching, any inkling they were doing something they shouldn't having been drowned by the mouthwatering notion of a Victorian sponge cake lying in wait on the kitchen table.

James cups his mouth blasting out two very loud goose honks. It seems all the children now use this call to announce their whereabouts. Done properly you can hear it over quite a distance. Paul responds and so does somebody else. Concrete reverberations place the second caller directly between the two houses each side of the alleyway. Paul runs to look over the bottom fence, honking as he goes. Clive has returned from wherever it is he has been and is available to play out. Shouting that "Carole is out," informs James he is wasting his time. He disappears from off his perch and Paul greets Clive with a suggestion. As it's blustery Paul proposes visiting the high-rise flats to play in the forceful gales that whip around them. He's still a little cautious after being swept away on a strong gust the last time he attempted to fly, but undeterred. They take turns using Clive's coat. Unfortunately the wind is not as gusty as he thought and after a few disappointing glides, which are actually more like extended leaps, Paul hands back Clive's duffle coat and they abandon the flight training.

Be it winter or summer, Paul rarely passes by the flats without spending a moment bathing in the hot scented air of the laundry vents. Afterwards they head behind the shops for a good old mooch around the bins. Flipping and flashing amongst the litter in a windy tornado, a twisting blue note winks at Paul. In a split second his jolting heart recognises Her Majesty's smirk on a five pound banknote. Failing to capture this elusive image, first, second and third time around, it eventually claims him by sticking to his shin.

"Fuck-in' hell." His disbelief speaks and Clive responds.

"What? What is it? What ya found?"

"A fiver..." Paul's incredulous answer is whispered with the addition of a rather weak and shaky, "Yay!" His eyes dart about as he cautiously secretes it into his pocket. Instructing Clive to run, Paul gallops away to a secluded place he knows, a snail place. Behind a hedge, he slowly draws the note from his pocket, silently praying it *is* what he thinks it is. And it is.

"Lemme see!" Clive reaches out but not as quickly as Paul recoils. Sharpened instincts and perhaps greed fuel the swift curtness of, "Get off! I found it." Paul considers a while for he has never possessed so much money. This sudden change in circumstance provokes an internal struggle, or more a one-sided battle. Should he rush straight home and offer it up to his dad? Or maybe, perhaps keep it? Guilt doesn't often triumph over excitement so it comes as no great surprise that Paul decides to spend it.

Clive is not given half: in Paul's world things are rarely divided evenly. Instead after treating themselves to a bag of chips and a can of fizzy cola, he gives Clive a pound. Out of the change he inserts two pence into a Dr Barnardo's collection box. This isn't an act of charity nor is it a sign of guilt, but an extravagant whim simply to entertain. Fondly he watches as the coin cascades along the zig-zag slopes before dropping out of sight. They return to the flight launching wall by the flats and allow the wind to cool the chips as they eat. Paul has often drooled, imagining himself devouring a big bag of chips. Lured by creeping vapours, like in a cartoon, he once sleepwalked down the stairs to the living room. His father, back from the pub, was tucking into cod and chips. When he asked what he wanted and questioned if Paul had wet the bed, Paul gave no response. He didn't know as he only woke up when he entered the room. Paul was told to fetch himself a plate and given some chips with a bit of fish.

Picnicking by the flats, Paul discovers that he actually prefers home-cooked chips to chip-shop ones. They don't leave a bitter taste clutching the sides of his tongue. He also finds out that, as much as he tries, he cannot drink a whole can of cola. Unaccustomed to bubbly pop his stomach bloats and produces so much froth that it enters his mouth whenever he burps. Clive, who is normally the bubble master supreme, cannot produce such a foaming mass but does deliver some rather impressive belches.

Passing by the flats on her way home from a morning of learning how to be a girl, Carole, alerted to a chorus of belched profanities and laughter, creeps up on the two noisy guzzlers.

"Oi greedy pig, where'd you get them? Can I have one?" A startled Paul pushes the bag into her hands.

"You can have em, I don't want anymore."

Carole appears grateful yet eyes them both suspiciously.

"I ay spat in em if that's what you'm finking," Paul assures her.

"No I know, I was just wondering who give ya the money."

"Found a fiver behind the shops." Clive's response, although honest, supplies more truth than is merited.

"A fiver? Ahh, you should have give it to Dad." Her accusing tone prompts a resurgence of guilt to drench Paul's glee. Disgrace, regret, fear and panic now wash over him.

"I'll give you this if you don't tell..." Paul attempts to entice Carole by flashing a fifty pence piece beneath her nose. Carole deliberates: her righteousness and loyalty are less corroded than Paul's.

"It's one of those special ones." Paul shows her the nine clasping hands on its tail-side. Wavering, she bites her bottom lip.

"Ok then." Suddenly snatching the coin, her face beams with delight. Paul then informs her that James from the children's home has been sitting on his fence honking and, as Paul hoped, Carole speeds off.

Clive and Paul visit the supermarket where they purchase a giant-sized box of matches. What more could a naughty kid wish for than two hundred and fifty red-headed strike-anywhere flaming rods. Well, in Paul's case, a greedy-sized bar of chocolate. As for Clive, another can of pop. Top Deck, fizzy lemonade and lager. Shandy especially marketed to children. Paul can't abide the taste of beer. He also hates gin. Bill once gave him some disguised as plain water and it made Paul instantly vomit. The two boys slowly slug along in the direction of home throwing struck matches into the air. Carried by the wind they are extinguished before they hit the pavement.

Over the back park, the vacant swings provoke an involuntary reaction to dash over to claim them, which they do. They spend a while swinging whilst standing up and then another, sitting still whilst eating chocolate and drinking shandy. Their last whiles are spent hunched over the seat, holding onto the sides and using their feet to spin around and around until the wound up chain crunches to a tangled halt. Lifting their feet allows the swing to unwind at an incredible rate of knots. Paul's stomach is wrung like a wet rag, making him feel quite queasy. The final jolt of the uncoiling swing persuades him to cease this twisted game.

Before they leave the park, and after many attempts, Clive and Paul manage to wrap their swing around the topmost bar of its frame. With a jump and then a hard downwards thrust, the swing's momentum carries it up and over to rotate many times. The motionless swing dangles out of reach and out of action. A sight toddler Paul previously whinged about when he and Carole repeatedly failed to shimmy up the slanted poles to unwind it. With contentment Paul views his achievement as another milestone in becoming one of the big kids.

With Clive's mother out visiting family and his father enjoying an afternoon beer at the local pub, Clive and Paul end up playing in Clive's back garden. What fun they have throwing lit matches into patches of dry grass, igniting small forest fires and watching them spread across a miniature landscape. Like antelope over an African plain, the ants and beetles scurry away from the flames' destructive path. When the blazes stretch a little too far, they are immediately stamped out in an excited panic. Hidden by the glaring sunshine within the black extinguished patches, the occasional glowing fibre rekindles but with hawk-eyed vigilance they soon detect them and easily smother them beneath dancing feet. After a while Paul says his goodbyes. Clive remains with a pocket of loose matches sitting atop the fence, flaming missiles continuing to fly.

Carole, James and a gathering of eight children are playing out in the street. Carole has spent her money on one of those contraptions. Standing far apart Carole and James are also opening and closing their arms sending a second oval ball whooshing along a cord. Just like Jessica Wright and Mandy Cropper, only Mandy has now been replaced by Debbie Murphy from five doors down. At first glance one might assume they are all playing together and after a frustratingly long wait Paul finally gets to have a turn.

"Carole, Paul, get here now!" Mark, shouting out of the living room window, appears to be annoyed. James tells Carole he needs to go deliver newspapers and waves goodbye. Carole scoops up the strings of her toy. Mark's initial anger at what he perceives to be a family betrayal of Carole and Paul playing with one of the Wrights is instantly redirected.

"Where'd you get that?" he enquires in an accusing tone.

"I bought it." Carole's directness causes Paul to bite his bottom lip and to deliver her a silencing glare.

"And where'd ya get the money from?" Mark's further questioning appears to be leading to Paul's downfall. Expecting Carole's answer to almost certainly drop him in it, Paul contemplates punishment for selfishly wasting the fiver.

"Mrs Green give it me, for babysitting." Carole's righteousness soon shows Mark. Still perturbed, though, he issues an additional warning to keep away from that Jessica Wright.

Paul discovers that Carole hasn't really lied, or not fully. Mrs Green had actually paid her a pound for looking after her child that morning. Concerned about being duped, Paul tries to renegotiate his original deal, stating that maybe the whizzing ball thing could be both of theirs. Handles tangled up with cords, Carole attempts to straighten out the strings. She fails miserably, and so does Paul. Ultimately after tugging and cutting, what is left is a rugby-shaped ball, four hand-grips and a knotted stringy mess.

Twenty minutes later the spectacle of a fire engine ticking over in the cul-de-sac draws Paul along with many other residents back out into the street. Firefighters rush with a hose into Clive's back garden, and seconds later hissing white bellows plume skyward and a stream of water flows down the path into the road. The firemen, making sure not a spark is alive, thoroughly drench the whole garden area, taking a good ten to fifteen minutes and using many gallons of water. Once the engine has pulled away the local residents are left with the smell of wet charcoal and Clive's fence is a blackened mess.

Chapter Twenty-Four: Street Sweeping

Fearing chastisement Clive and Paul observe the ominous figure of Mr Loft swaggering down the street. Being a tall, well-built man he is easy to distinguish even from a great distance. Clive normally shows no fear whenever his mother threatens to inform his father about his misdoings. "I doe care, tell him!" is a usual response to her warnings. Though never witnessed firsthand, Paul has heard that Mr Loft is reputed to have a heavy hand when it comes to disciplining his children. Up on his toes Clive looks ready to scarper, his face the colour of porridge. Neither of them moves. Side by side they remain to face the consequence of their actions.

It is a strange breeze that blows this day. Instead of irate words and rage, Mr Loft is calm, philosophical even. Pragmatic, his disappointment is expressed in a *c'est la vie,* kids of today kind of way. Before heading inside for a snooze, he issues a mild mannered lecture about selfishness, responsibility and using time constructively. This leaves Clive and Paul sitting on the front wall pleasantly nonplussed. They decide to make amends by showing they can behave unselfishly and so take to sweeping away the muddy wet sludge and traces of burnt grass left along the path by the fireman's hose. Then they proceed to pick up the rest of the litter on Clive's garden.

Virtuous sensations brought on by their actions inject them with a will to continue. Paul's front garden is next. It gets a general tidy-up, the dusty pathway left spick and span. Pleased with the results of their new pastime they stick at it. A section of pavement between Clive's and Paul's house, approximately one-third of the cul-de-sac, is next to be swept. The packed slots of a drain, blocked with dead leaves, mud and dandelions has created a fair sized puddle in the gutter. Clive uses the handle of his broom to poke and prod away the muck. Sucking and squelching and seeming like fun, Paul joins in and down the drain the water eventually runs. They collect sweet wrappers and other bits of litter lingering along the kerb. Pressing on, their brooms glide over the other two-thirds of the pavement to complete the circuit. In the middle of the road right in the centre of the circle, debris gathers in pot-hole crevices. This makes their clean-up appear somewhat incomplete. So they set about sweeping the tarmac surface too.

Even when the melody of the ice-cream van lures children into the street, they continue to sweep. Under normal circumstances Clive would have rushed into his house to seek out his mother and Paul would have hung around the van to ask for broken cornets. Yet despite the money in Paul's pocket they fastidiously plough on, heads down brushing, or, as Clive calls it, brooming. This doesn't go unnoticed. Clive's dad shouts over to them. He praises them for their efforts, suggests they take a break and rewards them with money for an ice-cream. They purchase two Screwballs, ice-cream in a conical cup with a bubble gum at the bottom and a drizzle of red syrup on the top.

Ginger Charley and Crybaby Kenny miss seeing but hear mention of the fire engine. They want to know all about the fire and ask if Clive and Paul have to sweep the street as punishment. Clive shrugs off the fire as if it were a non-event and gives them the impression that the road cleaning just needed to be done and that he and Paul are simply being neighbourly. Furthermore, he suggests they can't hang around chatting as they are eager to polish off their Screwballs so they can get right back to it. Charley and Kenny then request permission to join their cleaning crew, which is granted providing they go home to fetch their own brooms. Within half an hour four more children have been enlisted, making a total of eight sweepers. This soon swells to ten and then twelve. Like a bush fire, a blaze of brushes sweep up the street, and as teatime approaches almost every available child is outside, broom in hand.

When Paul goes in for tea his soft-bristled brush is almost worn down to its wooden head. His father isn't too pleased about that. Paul rather reluctantly presents his dad with a pound note. He tells him he found it whilst cleaning. Carole says nothing about the fiver. "That should come in handy," Dad says, placing the note in his back pocket. Paul, half hoping he'd be told he could have it, shows no sign of disappointment. He does, however, feel a warm wave of relief. One that douses those niggling sparks scorching his guilty conscience. Suspecting that his dad would have probably kept the fiver validates his initial decision to selfishly spend it.

The next morning, after drying the breakfast dishes, Paul takes up his worn-out broom and meets Clive someway up the road. It seems they have started a new craze. Glen and Pamela from the nearby grove are already brushing the pavements outside their home. Following behind them is a small toddler dragging a broom. By noon more children are involved. Those living in Shane's street, at the top of the road, have also taken up arms to battle against dust and detritus. The following day, Becky Harris and Wanda Davies from the council side of the main road begin sweeping too. Carole, her admirer James and Belinda from the children's home join the workforce. Without much exaggeration, and perhaps a little imagination, one could say the pavements in the local area gleam.

After a third day of questionably hard graft, Paul is suffering with aches and pains. He has a rash, his head is sore and he's running a fever. With low energy his weak legs haven't the strength to carry him down the stairs, so that morning he has to descend them on his bottom, one step at a time. It takes him a while. Concerned, his father sends him straight back to bed and a little while later Carole pops up to deliver him a hot drink. A special *magic* drink: watered down evaporated-milk heated on the stove, a spoon of honey from a jar kept on the top shelf and a dollop of his dad's butter. Paul remembers having this potion previously but it didn't make him retch as it does today. He can't drink it but Carole can.

A short time later Doctor Woods arrives. He gives Paul's belly a tickle and diagnoses his symptoms as chicken pox. He tells Paul's father to keep him in bed for the entire day. Furthermore, for fear of infecting others, Paul is strictly forbidden to play outside until the rash subsides. Paul curses his luck to get struck whilst school is out. Lying in bed he listens to the children playing outside in the sun, and although he can't hear much sweeping assumes that the clean-up operation is still going on. Small, irritating blisters pop up all over his body; his fingers, unconsciously drawn to them, rub and pick. Paul makes a small discovery: the mysterious lotion the Indian lady from next-door applied to his stings wasn't magical or witchical. It was, in fact, Calamine lotion or so its pink colour and sweet odour suggests.

After days and days trapped indoors, Paul, itching to get out, scratches at the window. Through it he watches a gathered crowd. A photographer and journalist from the local newspaper have arrived to cover a story. One about community spirt and neighbourhood pride. Mrs Wright, head of the tenants' association, is chatting away to the journalist.

An irate photographer, hoping to shoot the unruly mob, some of whom are wielding brooms, is directing his subjects into position. Standing at the rear amongst the tall people, Clive's father, his arms folded, strikes a bold pose. Wanda and Becky, front and centre, continue to jostle for a better position by elbowing Pamela and Glen to one side. Carole, struggling to maintain her somewhat painful smile, is there with James and Belinda. Crybaby Kenny and Ginger Charley are also there, as are Martin Murphy, his cousin Keith and older sister Debbie. Under the close supervision of his parents, classmate Shane is looking monstrously angelic. It was he who'd carried the baton slash broom, after it had swept around Paul's cul-de-sac and travelled up the street to the twins in the grove. He had joined in with much enthusiasm, passing by his abode to meet Wanda and Becky at the junction of the main road. On the very end of the camera's focusing frame, posing with jazz-hands and a massive smile, stands Clive, minus his duffle coat.

Paul is fuming at being deprived of the prestige of having his picture in the papers. All his endeavours to be a good boy are to go unrecognised. Adding to his annoyance are all the interlopers who didn't help, such as his big brothers Mark, Jason and Darren, Stephen also, all of whom did nothing. In fact, from the posing crowd of around forty, at least half were not included in the workforce. Watching those glory thieves, holding brooms and smiling, is an affront to his striven efforts.

Shane waves over at Paul. The photographer calls for semblance. Jessica Wright and her bossy mother manoeuvre into prime position, wedging themselves right in-between Wanda and Becky. Then, as history stands still, the moment, along with Wanda's crabby expression, is captured by the lens.

As the crowd begins to disperse, Paul properly frustrated and desperate for attention, stands on the windowsill calling out. Nobody, not even Clive, who shouts back, "O'm not allowed!" is willing to approach him for fear of contamination. Paul catches the children hollering about going to the park. He watches the street empty then slumps off to the dining room where his dad is sitting in his usual chair playing chess with himself.

Some days later the newspaper article, alongside a photograph of the entire sweeping brigade, appears on page five. Taking full credit for uniting the neighbourhood in a clean-up operation is Mrs Wright, chairperson of the tenants' association. Paul wishes he could have claimed his glory, tell everyone it was he who found the fiver that bought the matches that started the fire. That if it wasn't for him and Clive clearing away the debris after the firemen had extinguished the flames, it would have been just an ordinary, non-eventful six-weeks of holiday.

Perhaps this episode of neighbourhood unity is the reason nothing ever comes of the eviction petition to rid the street of its undesirable family. Or maybe the pressure was off due to Mrs Chadwick and company moving to another area. Whatever the reason, the attention of the tenants' association appears to be focused elsewhere.

Chapter Twenty-Five: Questionable Behaviour

Circumstance often creates victims out of impulsive attention-seekers and, as it is in Paul's nature to either zonk out into a daydream or disrupt the class to gain a laugh, his reading progress has dramatically slowed. Academically he is failing yet his popularity, as fickle as it is, is currently on the rise. Stunts such as swapping over the bottles of sour milk have given him a certain notoriety amongst fellow scallywags. He views leaving the door of his snail colony slightly open for an entire weekend as a stroke of pure genius. By Monday morning there are silver trails up the walls and some of the escapees are found hiding in the children's book-drawers. Mr Moody is far from amused at being greeted by the foul stench and slimy sight. It is over a fortnight before the last snail is rounded up. Paul, feigning ignorance, gets away scot-free although the colony and all its residents have to be put outside.

***

Now in Class Six with two years to go, Mr Barton, the PE instructor, has become his new class tutor. At six foot something, Mr Barton towers way above Paul's previous teacher, Ms Lammers. With his grouchy moustache and fierce gaze he can appear wildly menacing when angry. His booming voice can make a stone statue quiver to rubble and dust. Paul, testing his boundaries, soon learns that a slight sprinkle, in the form of a witty remark, will be tolerated, but long squirts of blue ink across the ceiling will not. Paul's class have progressed from writing with pencils to using fountain pens. Behind Mr Barton's desk, in a recess next to the door, is the filling station where pupils top up their spent ink cartridges using a somewhat dangerously sharp syringe and a giant bottle of Quink ink. Beyond Mr Barton's line of vision, providing he is sitting at his desk, the show-offs deliberately spurt ink overhead. Paul isn't the only one daring enough to add to the myriad of dotted lines that criss-cross the ceiling. Bobby, Shane and some of the girls, like Jenny Merrill and Lucy Pink, have also sprayed ink. Even the new posh kid, Andrew Gold, has made his mark. Yet it is Paul who gets the fright of his life, when, unbeknownst to him, Mr Barton happens to be standing beside him as he discharges a full syringe up the wall. The ensuing bellow catches Paul unawares. He is so shocked he unintentionally blurts in front of the whole class. However, it isn't fearful tears that issue forth, but profanities. The gasps of a gobsmacked class rock the desks as Paul tells Mr Barton to fuck off. He, in return, orders him to go and stand outside Mr Graham's office.

Paul is fast growing accustomed to the aroma of strong black coffee, and regardless of the imminent chastisement, he much prefers lingering about the staff corridor to the solitude of standing outside his classroom in an empty dining hall. He is content to watch the comings and goings where each swing of the staffroom door emits a fresh waft of percolating coffee beans. Occasionally a passing secretary might cast him a wry smile or a pupil off on an errand may stop to get the low-down. Today it is Martin Murphy from the street who hears about his bravery. Paul boasts about how he told big bad Mr Barton to fuck off.

Perhaps Mr Graham is becoming resigned or maybe he's concluded that corporal punishment in the form of slapped legs has no effect. Not for the first time this term, Paul gets away with an angry rant and rave. He's also ordered to spend his break time picking up litter, a new, liberal form of discipline which he views as a novelty.

Gathering discarded crisp packets and the like, Paul, in the company of Bobby and Shane, strolls the outer edges of the school playing fields. A football amongst nettles in a bordering garden tempts the children. Shane pulls at the bottom of the chain-link fence. The entangled grass rips away. Next he pushes aside the twisting brambles blocking the gap. Much too tough to break they spring straight back into place, their scratching prickles conjuring up a few choice words. Shane takes off one shoe to use as a glove. Holding back the vines with it, this allows Paul and then Bobby to squeeze underneath. Once inside the garden they quickly retrieve the ball and, after swiping a few apples, they exit the garden with their prizes. When filched, even the sourest of cooking apples taste sweeter. Or so it seems. Shane polishes off the bitter apples with bravado whilst Bobby and Paul debate who keeps the ball. Bobby wins with his assertive claim that he saw it first. So he gets the football, Paul gets a somewhat impressive X-shaped scratch on the back of his hand and Shane, he gets a bellyache.

When it comes to executing naughtinesses, a proficient Paul appears to fear no repercussions. There was a short period when a bad school report saw Paul and his siblings tremble. They would wait in a line at home, hands outstretched to receive a few swipes from a bamboo cane. His father would punish anyone who received an E, the lowest possible grade. One strike for each E. It wasn't uncommon for the three eldest to use matching coloured ink to round off some of their Es to make them look like Bs. But after countless bad reports of, 'could try harder', 'easily influenced' and 'lacks concentration', the futility of caning to produce better grades dawns on their father. Over the years, dealing with the establishment has left their dad with a *them and us* viewpoint that underlines intolerance. He can quite comfortably believe that the teachers simply don't like his kids. That they are biased and, to go even further, are purposely picking on his little imps. He no longer enquires about school reports and Paul is glad not to show them.

That's not to say that his bad deeds now go unpunished. On the contrary, their dad continues to enforce a strict regime within the house. The children undertake all chores without question and with no hope of a pocket money reward. Echoes of the same phrase "Cuz you 'aven't got a mom," persist in stifling any notion to voice a "But why?" Thankfully, Sergeant Major Bill has moved in with his latest fling so dusty finger-swipes from his inspections no longer smudge reddened cheeks. Nevertheless, their father must be satisfied with the housework before allowing the children to play out. In the house, when their father is about, the children generally display wings and wear a golden halo. Once out of sight these are replaced with horns and a pointy tail. The notion of 'harmless fun' and remarks such as 'just kids messing about' mean that few restrictions are placed upon the children. They are more likely to be chastised for the careless stupidity of getting caught than for the actual deed of stealing sweets. However, answering back is never tolerated, even a frustrated sigh can be punished. No waste, respect the elderly and no hitting girls covers pretty much everything.

Despite the lack of rules and the simplicity of the few there are, Paul seems prone to learn his lessons the hard way. Threatening his sister Carole with a dinner fork, for instance. He won't be doing that again in a hurry.

The incident happens on a normal-ish Sunday. His pigeon-racing father is out attending a meeting at a pub called the Bradshaw Arms. Carole and Paul have peeled the potatoes ready for lunch, and although the children were told not to go out, the house is empty. As standard, the three eldest are playing over Windsor Park. From there they can look across the fields, through the playground of a local school and recognise the distinctive strut of their father as he makes his way home along the main road. Running at full pelt, which is required as their dad walks quicker than any other dad they know, they arrive home and sit enthralled in whatever it is they are pretending to do. Often, and providing they have a TV set at the time, one of them will check the programme listings then excitedly chat about how great the show is.

This Sunday is classed as normal-ish because, on this rare occasion, the special treat of a lime jelly is setting in the fridge. It is the fingerprints that someone has pressed into the jelly's surface that makes Paul misbehave the way he does. Frightened by the repercussions when denials come from all quarters, he decides Carole should be the one to own up. So he attempts to persuade her using a dinner fork pressed to her neck. When the jelly imprint issue is broached, Carole mentions the fork incident. This incenses their father immensely and, since the previous one has vanished in a puff of bonfire-smoke, Paul is commanded to go fetch a stick from the garden. He returns with the thinnest bamboo cane he can find.

Holding out his right hand, knowing what is to come, tests Paul's mettle. Refusal isn't an option, compliance the quickest solution to end the ordeal. He braves the first stinging strike with a sharp intake of breath and a quick shake of the hand. It is a quivering hand that receives the second blow. Whoosh, how easily the stick cuts through the air to find its mark. Paul exclaiming "Ow, ow, ow!" dances on the spot, pressing his hand between his knees. He takes the third hit on his other hand, by which time tears have cleared pathways along both cheeks. The fourth falls suddenly to a dithering hand that buckles a fraction before being struck. Luckily his father appears unaware and turns his attention to Mark, who was left in charge. He receives a scolding too for not putting a stop to Paul's threatening behaviour.

As naughty as Paul is, or isn't, menacing behaviour and telling lies don't sit comfortably with him. A niggling suspicion that disapproving glances are being cast from beyond the clouds pricks at his conscience, and when a lull in life's chaos allows him to consider his actions, he is never short on empathy. That said, Paul's roguish conduct is quite typical of a deprived child. Covetous, inadequate and consumed with social anxieties, he conceals his vexations behind the might of his centurion comrades. The defunct Social Scroungers has been rebranded: The Centurions are now in control, Roman soldiers from the previous year's Christmas nativity. Bobby, Shane and Paul, as well as a few others like Barry, who no longer bites, and Anthony Hayes, kids enlisted after the school play, march around the playground with a domineering deportment. Out of all the gangs Paul has been involved in this is surely the finest. Nobody messes with The Centurions. When playing British Bulldog, a game where the children must run from one safety zone at the far end of the playground to another at the other, The Centurions slowly march. A stern warning of "Touch me and I'll batter ya" does not diminish the fun in this chase-based game.

To specially selected non-members, offers of protection allow them safe passage, providing they walk alongside their guards. Paul escorts Andrew Gold, the new boy, with a spring in his step. Andrew has sheepishly, under duress from his parents, donated his old sports shoes to Paul: Nike trainers with foam-wedged waffle-soles. These are received with silent gratitude yet worn with thundering pride. Nothing feels quite like them. Paul bounces contentedly along on soft cushions. He articulates his unvoiced thanks by assuring his mates that posh boy Andrew is actually *all right*. Plus, he's been to America, which comes with the added prestige of him being the only child in school who has been on an aeroplane. Thankfully not one of the planes that Paul stares at, wishing it would fall out of the sky. One he'd run to, over the playing fields of Windsor Park, and where he'd find lots of valuable things lying about. His visions fortunately neglect to include any details of such a gruesome reality, unimaginable as it is to an uninformed child such as he. Paul's imaginings wholly include long swaying grass and sunshine. Open luggage strewn about, wallets full of cash and random good stuff, mainly toys, dotted about the fields.

After escorting Andrew to a secure location, Paul, making his fifth crossing, is seized upon by the catcher, Derek Cole. Narked by the audacity Paul, without much thought, boxes him on the nose, which in turn dribbles red. Paul's face flushes white with worry because, as those around him know, blood equals seriousness. The headmaster listens to Paul's fabricated explanation and is convinced that being swung around and crashing to the ground merits a reactionary blow. So, once again, Paul returns from his office dry-eyed with a puffed-up nonchalance befitting a brave centurion.

Despite praying nightly, the needle in Paul's moral compass gyrates erratically as though it's gone haywire. It fluctuates between sinful and saintly with a strong leaning towards the roguish. Religious preachings about the commandments, heavenly virtues and deadly sins appear to him to be open to interpretation. Fragments gleaned from news reports regarding the conflict in Ireland, supported by priests on both sides, leaves his father speechless enough to make a speech. A long one, where the words "hypocrites" and "holy" are uttered with contempt. Stories about mafia wars often portray savage murder as unfortunate incidentals. Catholic teachings proclaim these sins can be absolved with a confessional-box pardon. Possessing a Catholic identity means Paul and his school friends revere rather than condemn these villainous organisations.

With the assistance of Shane, his henchman, the two of them set up a 'kind donations scheme'. A charity of sorts, where their classmates can, if they so wish, contribute items to poor and needy children. Namely Shane and Paul. They don't issue threats of violence, just strong, persuasive appeals with a slight hint of menace. They amass quite a hoard: sweets and fruit, pencil-case items and football cards, as well as toys such as Matchbox cars, marbles, and clackers, which are all the rage. Two hard plastic balls attached to a length of string, that, with the right technique, clack together above and below the hand. They make a horrendously loud clatter, dangerously alarming for parents, and the balls bruise and batter and sometimes shatter into sharp flying fragments.

Whenever possible the two divide everything they collect fifty-fifty. From the spoils Shane picks a game called Jack Straws. Small plastic items shaped like ladders, saws and garden forks that must be extracted, without disturbing the pile, using a little hook. Paul chooses Mousie-Mousie, a game where the players place their coloured mice nose to nose on a small, round mat. Holding them by their long tails they wait for the catcher to roll a coloured-dice. When blue or red show on the dice, the catcher's hand, holding a plastic cup, swoops down hoping to catch those too slow to pull away. It is a simple type of fun that creates much joy and laughter, until the tails snap off thus ruining the game.

They strictly adhere to this agreement of going halves until the ultimate betrayal. Someone gives Shane a chewy Refreshers sweet. One that could, with a little tugging and lots of dribble, easily have been bitten in two and shared. Instead he shoves the whole thing into his greedy gob. Paul, who's inherited some of his father's knee-jerk principles, dissolves their mafia partnership quicker than Shane's saliva does the sugary chew.

Regardless of outward impressions, Paul, the boy who rescues worms, isn't entirely suited to a life of gangsterism. His decision only affects their racketeering alliance, not their friendship. That remains the same. They continue to walk to school together and at break times bounce around in the playground. Centurion soldiers previously members of the Social Scroungers, who were formerly known as the Anti-Creeps. Shane never joined the Scrumpers' Union as his parents continually forbade him to play with the roughnecks down in the cul-de-sac.

Much to the delight of staff members assigned to playground duties, The Centurions get the perfect opportunity to buff-up their tarnished reputations. Once everyone has eaten lunch, some of the older children from Class Seven are tasked with stacking chairs and putting away the dining tables. However, when the sun shines the helpers often shirk their duties, preferring to play football. Bobby, Shane and Paul, who normally wait for seconds, are often the last to finish eating. Therefore, when the kitchen staff discover the older students have absconded, the three from Class Six jump at the chance to offer up their services.

Paul sees lugging around tables and chairs as an extension of play. It's much more exciting than running behind a rush of children all chasing a tennis ball that is too small to kick. Stacking and dragging furniture into the storeroom soon becomes a daily occurrence. After a while, the simplicity of it does become a tad tedious, then Paul finds himself doing much the same thing as the other kids out in the playground: playing football. A new game, invented by Bobby called crazy-football where mis-kicks and odd bounces are the biggest part of the fun. The gummy protection caps from the end of the table legs become the ball and the door to the store room, the goal. Nigh on impossible to score, these rubber stoppers ricochet at awkward angles that it's hopeless to predict. The cap rolls in wide arcs across the polished wooden floor. In stockinged feet the parquet surface becomes extremely slippery. The result is extra long skids, some rather dramatic collisions and a great deal of raucous laughter. When up to no good, excited rapscallions often produce more noise than is wise. A double dare from Paul to Shane becomes a triple dare from Shane to Bobby. Bobby then ace dares Paul to remove the pin and squeeze the lever of a small black fire extinguisher behind the storeroom door. The lightest pressure on the handle emits a deafening burst of carbon dioxide. A blast that is ever so thrilling if not somewhat scary. This also becomes a daily occurrence. Neither polished nor sullied, the boy's dubious reputations manage to remain exactly the same during this brief period of helpfulness. Then as springtime shifts into summer they also decide, like the children of Class Seven, that despite their lunchtime antics, rolling down the ditch in the sunshine is much more fun than stacking furniture. Avoiding their duties comes at a cost, one felt by their bellies. They miss out on seconds every time they slope off after lunch.

Chapter Twenty-Six: Thus Far

Thus far, Paul's formative lessons have warped his outlook on life. He is developing a sizeable wedge on his shoulder. Those whom his dad often refers to as *them* appear to have all the cream, whilst he is left with water from the tap. *They* are numerous and seem to include everyone who isn't part of Paul's family. "It's one law for them and it's another for us." His father's rhetoric has little time to simmer when Paul's own frustrations, about being an *us,* continue to bubble over. Each unfulfilled want and need scorches his somewhat thin-skinned existence. Not that Paul can comprehend the finer points of social Darwinism. News reports about proposed welfare reforms go way over his head. The general gist of his father's gripes is that politicians, unrestricted by the rules they set, flourish in a nepotistic environment where corruption is rife. Out of touch with the common man, they live in towers of ivory. Deeds, consequence and responsibility are but platitudes often heard yet rarely observed. Be it a sex scandal, an attempted murder or a fake suicide, their wrongdoings appear only to be addressed when witnessed or challenged.

Within his household the general consensus is that the figures of authority who make judgements and prosecutions are viewed as two-faced antagonists who legislate against the poor but never their own. From the snippets he hears, Paul has managed to deduce that owning-up is for numskulls. All those silly rules. Keep off the grass! No ball games! Trespassers will be prosecuted! Paul flouts them as a matter of principle. In his eyes only God has the right to pass judgement and although it's no guarantee, it is the promise of a heavenly paradise, where he can eat bananas every day, that holds tightly onto Paul's lead. Forgiveness for his minor transgressions such as scrumping, thumping and the occasional fib he negotiates through prayer. Wheeling and dealing with an almighty entity not nearly as strict as preachers like to make out.

God has become a good friend and ally to Paul. Over the years Paul has shared intimate secrets, cried, and on the odd occasion, mostly around Christmas time, rejoiced in the tangible gifts of life. Paul is confidently assured that *He up there* knows what lies inside him isn't entirely wicked.

Always questioning, Paul decides what is moral and which doctrines to believe. Does the Lord recognise the ownership of land and that of an apple hanging from a tree? Paul thinks not. What about a captive bird? Is it still one of God's creatures or does it belong to man? Whether or not Paul is attempting to be a righteous Christian, opportunities to stray from the path are plentiful under this method of self-governance. In the past Paul's questions regarding his virtue were fashioned in such a way that not appearing at the foot of his bed was an indication the all-powerful, ever-vigilant creator wasn't at all offended. God's failure to materialise thus gave the green light to many wayward deeds. Sometimes, after the fact.

Paul's recent confirmation means, just like the mafia, that redemption can still be his providing he's brave enough to admit his wrongdoings to the presiding priest waiting for his confession. Having his slate wiped clean polishes Paul's soul. His footsteps fall much lighter, his breaths taste cooler and a heavenly sense of renewal remains with him for a good part of the day. Martin Murphy and his sister Debbie attend confession every Saturday morning, without fail. On occasion, Paul asks if he can accompany them. On entering the church he anoints himself with holy water and feels much the better for it. He genuflects in front of the altar as a mark of respect and then takes a pew until it is his time to enter the curtained stall. Fighting the urge, his eyes cannot help but be drawn upwards to the grotesque figure of Jesus nailed to the cross. Paul is alarmed by such a sight. The sheer agony etched on Christ's face provokes much sympathy and yet, at the same time, repulses him. His confession about being horrible to Carole, scrumping and telling lies is merely a gesture to be given a penance. Saying one Our Father, three Hail Marys and a Glory Be restores his spirit to a more angelic state.

It has been a while since Carole and Paul visited Mrs McGaveridge. The last time they rang the doorbell, her son answered and sent them away rather abruptly. A pang of humiliation escorted them off the premises. Carole then decided, and Paul rapidly agreed, they were getting a bit too old for cadging pocket money anyway. And like most decisions Paul makes in haste, the regrets linger. Now whenever he passes by the church, an urge to call, just one more time, is halted by his developing red-faced awareness.

Obtaining money is never easy. Finding fivers happens but once in a childhood. Paul is too young to get a newspaper round like the one his brothers used to have. Last spring on Carole's birthday, Mrs Hodges failed to call with her fifty pence pieces. Paul had seen riding her bicycle up the hill near the high-rise flats. He shouted hello but she didn't appear to hear so he chased after her. Paul suspects she may have pedalled quicker because as fast as he ran, he couldn't catch up to her.

On those days when the sun blazes in a cloudless sky, Clive and Paul venture further afield. They visit the canal some three miles away, a day trip that costs no money but only time, of which they have plenty. There they can dip their toes in the murky green flow, skim a few stones and build a fire. Today, they take with them an old newspaper, two potatoes and a portion of tin-foil left over from wrapping the Christmas dinner. This is a repeat occurrence that always results in the same outcome. A lot of huffing and blowing to get the fire going, then a long hungry wait of anticipation with a discussion regarding cooking time. Following this, a struggle to manoeuvre the potatoes from the flames and another one to pick up the scorching hot delights that await them. Unwrapping the blackened tinfoil reveals a briquette of charcoal. When bitten the sooty skin unmasks a hardened core, which is as raw as when it was first dug. These are then lobbed into the canal as food for fishes.

After an unsuccessful attempt at scooping up some of the sticklebacks by hand they take a paddle in the shallow waters of an overflow channel. They see a barge puttering slowly towards them so they rush to put on their shoes and socks and run along the towpath to greet it. As they approach, a small dog drowsing upon the flat roof stirs. It stalks back and forth, viciously yapping, warning them not to get too close to the floating home. The woman steering is much more friendly. Clive wants to open the gate of the lock that will allow her boat to sail up the hill. She hands him the lock-key, much to the displeasure of the dog who, she assures them, has a bark that is much worse that its bite. The barge enters the lock through the lower gate which is already open. Pushing it closed takes the efforts of both of them. The barge waits in the bottom of the lock; wet walls green with slime tower above on either side. Canal locks are said to be extremely dangerous so Clive and Paul don't mess about. They rush up to the second gate. Turning the winding-gear, which also requires the strength of both children, allows the paddles to be lifted. Water then gushes into the walled chamber making the barge rapidly rise within the lock. Once the water level within is equal to that outside, the second gate can be opened to let the boat float out and onwards on its journey.

When Clive gives back the key, the angry mutt snaps at his arm, missing it by a mere whisker. Clive's reaction is too swift for the old dog but he drops the heavy metal key right on the lady's foot, causing her to squeal and the dog to yelp. Clive also lets out a brief exclamation, sounding like something between a snicker and a sneeze. Gulping back his own chuckle Paul thinks that will teach you for pretending your dog doesn't bite. Of course, he doesn't say so but Clive knows what his sidewards smile implies. Then the woman hobbles off to fetch a reward. She hands them two large carrots and gives them an apology for not having anything more suitable for a couple of very polite young children. The next five minutes are occupied with sitting in the sunshine, chomping and bunny impressions accompanied by "Neh! What's up, Doc." Hissing from their pissing, the smouldering cinders are extinguished and, just to be extra sure, learning from recent mistakes, Paul kicks the remaining embers into the water. Typically on ordinary days like today not much happens, and with nothing else to do they make their way towards home.

The lazy day heat shows in their languid pace as they wind their way back along the country lanes. When they return to civilisation, roads with pavements, they try their luck ringing the doorbells of large private houses to ask for a drink of water. In a pretence of being extremely thirsty, they force down glass after glass of unwanted tap water. Then they try the next house, hoping this time they will be given fizzy pop. By the time they receive the sugary drink they crave, they are too bloated to enjoy it.

They are aware of the dangers that strangers pose. A public service information broadcast on the television, one in which a supercilious cat named Charlie says, "Don't talk to strangers," has taught him to be aware of unfamiliar men, especially those with puppies. One kind gentlemen did invite them inside. They told him they're not allowed. Paul reckons he is much too wise to be murdered. Despite this, Clive and Paul have twice thumbed a ride home. One woman who drove them asked what they would do if she suddenly turned off and headed in another direction. Paul didn't give an answer, instead he fumbled in his pocket for his tiny penknife, just in case. A real stranger once pulled up alongside Paul asking for directions. Paul pointed down the road and the man asked if he could show him. Paul said there was no need to show him as the place he enquired about was just at the end of that road. The man then drove away. Paul decided he was most definitely a murderer.

One time Carole answered a ringing telephone in a public phone-box. Paul, sharing the handset, could hear the voice of a man on the other end. He started to ask them questions, such as where they were going and if they wanted to come for tea and cakes. The lure of cakes slightly tempted Paul but Carole, who had the impression the man may have been watching from a window above the chip-shop, yelled, "Quick! Murderer!" and slammed down the receiver. Then they ran away screaming, convinced they'd just had a lucky escape.

Paul is growing into a wise kid of the streets. No longer fearful of dressing gown shadows or the deaf girl up the road. Paul, once afraid of many things, grows a little braver and more resilient with age. When school resumes for his final year in Class Seven, he will be one of the big kids. Paul reckons it high time he grew up. He has been telling himself to do this ever since he prematurely quit giving his dad goodnight kisses many, many sleeps ago. He continually struggles to combat the infantile manner in which he sometimes speaks. With his peers, he chats with the ordinary enthusiasm of a nine-year-old, yet when around his elders he regresses to a cutesy voice. The switch between the two talking styles was hardly noticeable previously, but as Paul ages the change appears more pronounced.

Smoking fags, kissing girls and stealing are some of the things that his brothers do, so Paul decides he must now follow suit. He has recently begun to explore smoking by lighting up dog-ends picked out of the gutter. Clive also collects cigarette butts from out of his parents' ashtray. Paul's dad smokes his right down to the filter and, unlike Clive, Paul hasn't the audacity to steal one from his father's packet. Although once he was tempted to swipe a half smoked fag left resting in his ashtray. Recollections of a discarded frostbitten packet make Paul continuously check over the low wall near the shops. It is a convenient place for sitting and waiting, which means he can generally find some worthwhile stubs scattered there. Paul hardly coughed on his first draw, whereas Clive choked, spluttered and turned as red as a ripe cherry.

Being a year younger than Paul seems more significant to him now that he is contemplating joining a senior school in one year's time. Kissing girls, for instance: Clive may be proficient in running, jumping and climbing but he hasn't even pecked a girl on the cheek, whereas Paul has already kissed Jenny Merrill and snogged Pamela, the twin from up the road. Only last week she agreed to be Paul's girlfriend. Paul likes her because she always has warm hands and smells clean, like a bar of soap. She is also, in his opinion, an excellent kisser. When Clive and the other children play gutters in the street, she and Paul sit on the wall canoodling and holding hands. Regardless that Paul hasn't a notion of what the deed entails, he brazenly asks if she fancies a bonk. Pamela says, "No thank you." So they stick to kissing. Which actually suits Paul just fine. This summertime romance is due to last for roughly two weeks in which time Paul will eat a lot of Pamela's sweets.

Stealing? Paul is still getting to grips with the finer points regarding the rights, and the wrongs of it. He often concocts justifications for his actions to ease his uncertainty. Bottles of milk left on doorsteps will only turn sour and get wasted. Grapes growing in a glasshouse, accessed through a gap in the alley fence, are fruit, a gift from nature, and so accordingly belong to all mankind and can be pinched. Even more loosely, when the old storekeeper near his school is occupied serving Shane, it's OK to swipe one or two penny sweets. Hidden behind his sweet smile, he dares not talk or allow his nose to betray the sourness of the cola-bottles tingling his tongue. Shelf upon shelf displaying jars of confectionery, bonbons sold by the quarter pound — what the old man doesn't miss surely can't hurt. Therefore, this crime is categorised as a minor infringement. One which can soon be forgiven, providing Paul has the nerve to disclose it to the priest taking confession. Similar to the rules of any game, Paul views all laws, be they earthly or divine, as guidelines which can easily be amended providing no one suffers. A patient Lord listens to Paul's prayed reasoning and, as Paul expects, expresses no disapproval.

Chapter Twenty-Seven: Budgies

The six-week holidays are over and a smell which Paul associates with the beginning of school, plus the end of fun, fills his bedroom. Brand new leather shoes and never-worn uniforms mix with the aroma of factory packaging. The scent of the Red House, a school outfitters store in town. Paul lays out a pair of long grey trousers on the bed. Above them he unfolds a red V-neck pullover to create a profile of how smart he will look. Using his teeth he tears an opening in the plastic packaging of a white cotton shirt. Inserting his index finger, he rips open the wrapping to withdraw the tightly pressed item and, with great care, he proceeds to extract the first of twelve metal pins. The shirt unfolds a little more with each extraction. He removes pins, plastic grips and cardboard bits that keep the collar in shape. A slight prick from an undiscovered thirteenth pin leaves a teensy spot of blood around the back tail. Not large enough to worry about, yet annoying enough to mar Paul's mood of complete readiness for his final year at primary school.

This year there is no duffle coat but there are some desperately needed shoes, for which Paul is grateful. Stained with mud, moss and soot, his Nike trainers are worn to tatters. The left one has a flapping mouth and there's a hole directly above his big toe on the right one. Once loved, these sports shoes are no longer suitable for anything and will, before long, be furnishing the feet of a Guy Fawkes effigy. All the same, until Bonfire Night arrives, they will be worn, and worn out, a while more.

Nearing pension age, Mrs Turner, Paul's latest teacher, has elephant lines around her eyes and crocodile skin covering her hands. Throughout the day, when the children pore over their books, she applies lotions and creams which she rubs into every crease. As pleasant as the ointments smell, Paul finds her slathering distracting, which is rich coming from Class Seven's chief disruptor. Mrs Turner is a very patient teacher, who seems to have a great deal of tolerance when it comes to Paul's random outbursts. When Paul's mind drifts through the drizzle outside the windows, becomes absorbed in a daydream or mesmerised by the scavenging gulls squawking near the kitchen bins, Mrs Turner, happy to let wayward wolf wander on, doesn't throw a blackboard rubber. With her Paul finds an upside to being a troublesome influence, a perk for being naughty: he's often bestowed with errands that take him out of the classroom.

Ten minutes before the lunchtime bell sounds, whilst the rest of the class are engaged in gaining an education, Bobby, Shane and Paul are sent out early to attend to their special duties. On the advice of Darren, who had done the same as Jason and Mark before him, Paul has used his father's pigeon-owning credentials to secure the position of chief budgie boy. Cutting class is payment enough to make Paul forget his aversion to dust and the things emitted by the preening shakes of puffed-up birds. There's the further incentive of a book token at the end of the year for performing the effortless chore of muck scraping, husk blowing and water changing.

Retrieving the aviary key from the secretary's office, the trio head to the infant's playground. Paul relishes his new sense of purpose, and the responsibility and the prestige that goes with it. Gathering around as they wait for lunch, the young ones mill about where the aviary encroaches on a small corner of their playground. Wide eyes gawping through the chicken wire, they admire the students from Class Seven. Always happy to chat, the budgie boys receive sweets which have been saved just for them, without even asking.

The boys perform their duties diligently and there is hardly any messing about. When accessing the enclosure, they must first enter the outer door and ensure it is closed behind them before opening the second, internal door. This way the children can cross the threshold without any birds taking flight. It is difficult to keep an accurate account of bird numbers. Amongst the flashes of green and pale blue flickers, the golden yellow flares and silver grey feathers, there are around twenty or so birds continuously flitting about. Paul's favourites are the twins, two pure yellow budgies with deep red eyes. From leafless branches suspended by wires and through reflections in their mirrors, the swinging birds look on from their high vantage points, observing the bustle below. The boys check nesting boxes for eggs, replenish birdbaths and reattach any fallen cuttlefish bones and millet stalks. The budgies are then left to perch and preen in peace and the aviary key is promptly returned to the secretary's office.

***

The budgie boys, aka The Centurions, decide they need to start training in preparation for senior school. In the next school they believe that children need to be able to brawl because running battles between rival secondary schools are commonplace. Fighting becomes part of their recreation. At home-time Bobby, Shane and Paul head to the nearest primary school. They wait, out of sight of the parents that congregate at the entrance, to try to pick a fight with students as they leave. Spitting, shoving and shouting abuse, purposely bumping into kids, warning them to watch where they're going, they quickly get chased away by some irate mothers. And because none of them wants to get into trouble, they quit this foolish activity after one lone attempt. Instead they return to wrestling one another, giving dead-leg punches and playing slaps.

Slaps isn't Paul's forte. A speedy game in which two competitors, hands flat as though in prayer, stand facing one another. Fingertips to fingertips, one player tries to be brave and not flinch before the other one, the slapper, parts his hands to take a swipe. If the slapper lands one they continue on until they miss. Twitching in pretence to get the receiver to move by mistake is a big part of the tactics. Moving for no good reason is penalised with a much harder free shot. Paul's reflexes are too slow. When he plays this at home he normally quits with stinging red hands after failing miserably on both the avoidance and the slapping part.

Besides all the rough and tumble they still run around playing British bulldog and find time for a spot of footy, Bobby becoming more football crazy of late. Space permitting, when the grass is dry, like today, they take part in rounders' matches. Despite the small detail that they are using a mini cricket bat instead of the cylindrical wooden ones which are usual, posh boy Andrew tells Paul it is very similar to American baseball. Andrew, the batsman, stands poised to strike the ball. Paul, the backstop, is waiting behind ready to catch it should he miss. A bright spark dissolves into black as Paul almost loses consciousness. The cricket bat has struck him hard in the face on the backswing. The sudden shock and excruciating pain makes Paul wail like crybaby Kenny. He gets escorted to the sickbay where the nurse dries his tears and stems the flow of blood. Made to lie down with a cold damp cloth over the wound, Paul falls asleep. A fair recompense for the stress, he misses the remainder of the day's lessons.

Overnight Paul's top lip balloons and blackens. Repulsed by his own hideous appearance he resents Andrew for making him more grotesque. An urge to take revenge conflicts with the knowledge it was only an accident and, besides that, Paul's gratitude for the sport shoes given him remains intact. The mirror in his hand reveals a pasty white face with a gaunt expression, scraggly long hair and something that resembles a black slug sucking on his top lip. Vanity casts a sad reflection as he dwells on this new image.

"Oi, shift it." Bill, the now none-of-the-time lodger, is visiting with his latest female friend and, as usual, throwing his weight around. Paul reluctantly relinquishes his seat on the couch. "You can stick the kettle on while you're up."

"Do it yourself, you doe live 'ere no more."

Paul swiftly exits the room. Bill, fast on his heels, corners him by the back door.

"I'll give you another thick lip if you're not careful."

"Go on then, try it, I ay scared of you." Paul picks up the nearest thing to him, a metal mop bucket. His whole demeanour is sullen and something in it tells Bill to back down, which he does. Previously Bill would have walloped him and sent him to bed without any tea. Something must have changed. Maybe Bill is frightened or perhaps he's been told he can no longer hit the kids, no matter what. Facing up to Bill is something of a milestone. Brave or stupid, he's been put in his place and Paul, once away from the house, feels all the better for it regardless of the dark clouds spitting down on what is turning into a miserable day. Clive is no longer available to play: his family are in the process of moving away. Paul consoles himself with the notion that he would have had to stop playing with him anyhow. After this final year Paul will be in senior school and Clive still in primary.

Paul tries to befriend another boy, one who lives over the back park in the house closest to the jungle gym. A lad closer to his own age. Sitting atop the climbing frame in his orange kagoul, munching on a bar of chocolate in the drizzling rain, Paul climbs up to chat.

"Off! This is mine." The boy lays a claim to the jungle gym. Paul continues to ascend the ladder ignoring his initial rudeness.

"Give us a bite of ya chocolate." Paul's request is met by a closed wrapper being shoved into the boy's pocket. Then the boy slips over the top bar, hangs and drops down to the ground. Paul does the same.

"Go on, just one, pleeeeease." Paul knows that adding an extra-long please sometimes works. Instead the boy gives him a shove. Paul's bottom hits the deck. Indignant, he jumps up and pushes the lad back. The boy, who has the girth of a chubby gorilla, gives Paul a second shove that sends him stumbling backwards once again onto the ground. This time when Paul gets up he punches the boy hard on the chin. The boy doesn't even flinch. Nor does he cry; instead, he thrusts both hands into Paul's chest delivering him into a heap on the floor for a third time. Paul is startled by the ineffectiveness of his hardest punch and weary of the boy's strength. Shamefaced and with a wet arse he walks away. The lad, nonplussed, climbs back to the top of the jungle gym, fishes out his chocolate and continues to munch. Excluding with his brothers, Paul has never lost a fight and this makes him anxious. He concludes that playing rounders instead of improving his fighting skills was a huge mistake.

***

It is true that initially Paul's budgie boy duties are performed without mischief. Typically, this doesn't last further than mid-October. Showing off his smoking prowess, Paul, away from the view of infants who may tell, puffs out a long plume of tobacco smoke into the air. He hands the cigarette to Shane who draws on it then violently coughs. Bobby, unimpressed, declines. This is not the result Paul hoped for. He thought it would underline his maturity and highlight the advancements he is making towards becoming a secondary school pupil. Instead, Bobby's forthright response that smoking kills has the exact opposite effect. It also makes him feel somewhat stupid and, for the briefest moment, detect a widening between them.

Not dwelling for more than a minute, they complete the daily chores of cleaning out the aviary and replenishing the food dispensers. This is still done to a satisfactory standard although much of the seed is now thrown over the adjoining fence. Another trick Paul has learned from his brothers.

When the seed runs out, two of them are permitted to visit the pet shop, unsupervised. A legitimate excuse to skive or play truant, as some people call it. Should they bump into PC Spoon on their travels, they have a genuine reason for being out of school. With this they can dawdle, within reason, and savour each and every liberated second. Paul is well acquainted with the store as he's been going there for such a long time. Most of his earliest memories of it have faded along with his nappy rash. Purposely he steps, leading Bobby past the empty hutches and wicker baskets that hold various sale items on the forecourt. With a customary pat he greets the blind dog standing guard outside the door. Not a blind dog like Blackie, his old labrador, this one doesn't fart: it can't, being a collection box made of clay. On entering the store the husky smell of bird seed and dried rabbit food welcomes Paul with a familiar wave. The shop's owner also acknowledges Paul in a similar way.

Paul, who invariably feels inferior due to constantly comparing himself with his peers, relishes the recognition and the brief discussion about not needing pigeon corn. He gleans a great deal of satisfaction from the storekeeper's familiarity with him, referring to his life out of school, and he welcomes the momentary intrusion provoked by the word, Dad. Image flashes of his father sitting in his usual chair by the gas fire watching the cricket. Paul's puffed-up ego straightens his posture.

Acting the oldest he's ever acted in his life, he allows a pensioner to be served first. This polite gesture, merely a ruse to lengthen his excursion from school, is appreciated with smiles and words of gratitude. With seed purchased they leave the store. Paul notices a pound note blocking the hole of the collection box, not quite sticking out though not yet fallen in. His attempts to extract the quid with his fingers fail. He looks around for a lollipop stick. Bobby's moral code won't allow Paul to steal from a charity box and he tells him so whilst pushing the note fully inside using a ring-pull from a drinks can. Maturity appears to come naturally to Bobby. Ever since he and Shane joined the school football team, which Paul views as a betrayal, he's developed a grown-up code of righteousness. Paul's grievances regarding this, and also the lack of loyalty they show when it comes to picking team members in PE class, remain unvoiced. Paul is conscious of being left behind. Subsequently he keeps secret from Bobby and Shane his following exploits.

Out that night with Darren and Jason, collecting wood for the bonfire, Paul produces the aviary key. He neglected to return it to the secretary's office that lunch time. It is Jason who suggests they go steal a budgie and, as Paul is included in this proposal, he agrees. His first real crime, as he sees it, thrills and frightens him. Rapids of blood pump through his veins. Making sure to stay out of sight of the caretaker's house, they vault the wall of the infant's playground. Swishes mix with hushes as their feet kick up a gathering of autumn leaves. Masking tiptoed steps, sounds from a nearby road rev up and die down. The chilled night air reveals Paul's excited panting. Keeping low, the three brothers scuttle along the boundary fence. It takes no time at all to open the lock and enter the cage. Darren inserts his hand into one of the nesting boxes, and, with a beak firmly grasping the webbed part of his thumb, he retracts his hand. Paul hears a few squawks from both Darren and the captured bird, although not so loud as to attract unwanted attention.

They arrive home with Saint Jude, the yellow budgie. It is the perfect crime. Their father is proud that his sons managed to rescue the poor thing from a cat in the alley. Delivered by Darren, his favourite son, he doesn't doubt this lie. The ironic name, Saint Jude, goes unquestioned too. At school nobody discovers that one of a pair, noticeable for being completely yellow, is even missing.

Paul continues to service the budgies every day. He tries to ensure the key is placed back in the secretary's key cupboard where it belongs at the end of each use. This he manages to do more times than not, although such a small thing is easily overlooked when rushing off to eat lunch.

Entering the aviary a few weeks later the boys discover a budgie dead on the floor. Shane suggests giving it a decent burial. They wrap it in a paper towel, and after bashing away at the frozen ground in a muddy corner of the schoolyard, lay it to rest. Shane, whose older brother is in training to be a priest, bows his head. Bobby and Paul join him in silent prayer. Ashes to ashes, dust to dust, they cover it with mud. To avoid discovery they decide against marking the grave. Inside the aviary Paul finds what he knows from experience: mouse droppings amongst the sawdust. Suspecting this may be the cause of the budgie's death, they develop an ingenious device to counter further attacks. A makeshift mouse-trap. Taking a plastic bucket filled three quarters of the way up with water, the boys add a large measure of strong disinfectant. Stinky stuff which they use to rid the place of mites. On top they float a layer of seed and leave the bucket in the closed section between the two doors so no budgies will get at it.

Proud at their own genius Bobby, Shane and Paul lock the door, convinced it will work. The next day they can't check because Shane took the key home and left it there by mistake. To ensure the birds don't go hungry they pour seed through holes of the chicken wire. The same thing happens the next day and the one after that because Shane can't find the key. On the fourth day Paul brings to school the large nail he used to keep in his treasure box. The budgies are in desperate need of fresh water and, as Shane hadn't found the key, he breaks in. He does it by twisting the nail in the clasp holding the padlock. The lock holds strong but the clasp snaps with ease. On the dusty floor lies another dead budgie, and in the death-trap bucket a hunched up mouse floats on the surface. They hold another funeral, once again presided over by Shane. The mouse and budgie are placed together beneath the earth but not before Paul exhumes the corpse of the first bird. He wants to even the odds to two budgies versus one mouse. Much fairer should a fight breakout underground. Paul then reports the burglary to Mr Graham, the headmaster. Inspecting the nail and clasp evidence, Mr Graham goes on to explain to Bobby, Shane and Paul how the thieves must have jimmied off the lock. Three budgies and one mouse down, the boys have fooled Mr Graham and Paul has gotten away with his first crime.

However, the three boys do not get the book token. Anthony Hayes, Derek Cole and posh boy Andrew are given it. Six weeks prior to their last day of school, Bobby, Shane and Paul are fired for matters unrelated to wasting seed, telling lies and burglary. Neither is it for lost keys. That had fallen in with Shane's PE kit and he eventually found it. In fact it is the simple act of laughter that becomes their undoing.

To young children with a keen sense of smell, onions can be quite amusing, comical as they are. Barry, the boy that used to bite, attracts their attention when they see him laughing hysterically. Pulling himself up to peer into the tall industrial bins behind the kitchens, Barry drops to the floor creasing up, holding his stomach with one hand, his nose with the other. Convulsions break out of him between his pained breaths. His highly addictive laughter draws them in. Then there are four children gripping the rim of the bin, staring down at onion papers to breathe in the pong. Rolling about in exaggerated agony and laughing way more than is merited. Out of bounds children should keep it down. Mr Graham gives no first or second warnings, instead he fires them on the spot.

Epilogue: Goodbye Saint Jude

So there we have a brief account spanning the first ten years of Paul's turbulent life. A social history report of a lower-class British family living in the 1970s. An exposé revealing the knock-on effects of growing up without a mother and the trials of being raised by a father who is struggling to cope. Paul, a daydreamy child who is also observant, has been sculpted by an impoverished environment that is harsh and lacking. His future has barely begun to unfold, yet academically he is failing, socially he is awkward, and his self-confidence remains fractured due to past events.

His days spent in care are a distant memory, a pleasant one where stripy toothpaste and breakfast cereal outweigh emotions regarding separation. Be it in jest or earnest, his father continues the threat of putting him into care whenever emotions run high. An official letter, a petition for divorce lodged by his mother, contains an additional clause. Carole and Paul are to be taken into care until Carole is sixteen, and furthermore Paul should remain there until he reaches the same age as his sister. They are both convinced by its authenticity though not at all worried. Paul will never reach the same age as Carole. It is revealed as a joke. An extra line of wobbly text has been added using the typewriter Jason had once salvaged from an empty house.

Christmas, the highlight of Paul's life, continues to bring him excitement and expectation, with an equal dollop of discontentment. Paul's unemployed father does his best to provide but money remains tight, and want aplenty.

It is difficult to ascertain what lessons Paul has gained from his early experiences. He is still struggling to read those wobbly lines of text that blur the more he concentrates. In his last school report, Mrs Turner said Paul must try harder. She also wrote that he is a bad influence and easily distracted. He doesn't look forward to senior school. Five lengthy years standing in between him and freedom. School is not for him. From day one, all he wants is to be finished. Perhaps Paul is wishing away the best years of his life, or maybe those are yet to come. As for Saint Jude the budgie? He was built a spacious cage out of an old fire guard and was free to fly around the room, perch on picture frames and poop in random places. He lived very happily for many years. Then, one fateful day, Paul is sitting on the floor in front of the leaky gas fire watching television. Totally consumed in an episode of Worzel Gummidge. One in which Worzel is off to a *Jumbly Sale* to buy a posh hat so that his beloved Aunt Sally will marry him. He swipes at the bird after it lands on his head. Not wanting any bird droppings in his hair, he only means to scare it. The poor bird must have been slightly dazed. It gets trodden on when Darren enters the room. The family have grown quite attached it by then and Mark, the eldest, even sheds a few tears as he attempts mouth-to-mouth and tries to squash it back into shape. Paul watches on. He confesses to nothing.

THE END

I hope you enjoyed these nostalgic reminiscences. A story made up using real events; a childhood very similar to my own. If you did, be sure to check out my other titles, Empty Corridors: Learning to Fail and Paulyanna: International Rent-boy.

Please leave a review. Reviews are worth their weight in gold and so important to indie authors like myself.